Legislativ

"Lobbying is a regul ... lobbyists, the Guide ... process and jump-start their successful careers; seasoned lobbyists will find the Guide to be both entertainment and a refresher course!"

Nancy Stephens, CAE, Executive Director
Florida Manufacturing and Chemical Council

"Having walked the halls of our Capitol for many years, I wish I had read this book before taking the first step. The details contained within are very revealing. I felt like I was privy to the most relevant information, like being in the locker room of an opponent learning how the game is really played. No assumptions, you'll know how to score."

Kathryn A. Parker, R.D., L.D.,
Former President and Legislative Chair
Florida Dietetic Association

"Bob Guyer has written the ultimate reference book for the newcomer and veteran alike on how to effectively lobby for one's cause."

James G. Cavanagh, Esq.,
Kelley Cawthorne

Guide To STATE LEGISLATIVE LOBBYING

By Robert L. Guyer

Published March 2000

Engineering THE LAW, Inc.
PO Box 35-7425
Gainesville, FL 32635-7425
ETLInc@learn-to-lobby.com.

Library of Congress Card Number: 99-91902
Main entry under title: Guide to State Legislative Lobbying

ISBN 0-9677242-0-1

Edited and co-authored by Laura K. Guyer, Ph.D.
Cover and book design by Michael Hoffmann

Printed in the United States of America.

This guide is dedicated
to advancing a government of the people
and for all the people by fostering the skills
that individuals and organizations need
to influence their state legislatures.

CONTENTS

PART II. Making Ideas Into Laws

Forward

Book stores are stocked with a wide variety of "How To Do It" publications, all aimed at helping a reader be successful in an area in which he or she has little or no previous experience.

Guide to State Legislative Lobbying plays that role in its area. For anyone thinking about trying to influence the outcome of a legislative proposal, a careful reading of the *Guide* will start the potential lobbyist higher up the learning curve and will accelerate the rate of progress.

An initial hurdle is whether even to try to do lobbying work. The term "lobbying" sometimes has a negative image, as if the practice is inherently unethical or improper. It is not.

Another fear is that, because of inexperience, the would-be lobbyist would not be successful. Nothing could raise the odds of success to 100%, but understanding and following the principles contained in this *Guide* will surely help.

Viewed another way, the *Guide* should encourage a person to work constructively with members of state legislatures on matters of public policy. That in itself would be a positive result.

In addition to having university degrees in political science, engineering, and law, Mr. Guyer has earned a Ph.D. in state legislative lobbying from the "School of Hard Knocks." During the years when he worked with state legislatures from coast to coast, Mr. Guyer met with Democratic Party majorities, Republican Party majorities, industry and public interest representatives, and others. In some instances, he worked in tandem with a local contract lobbyist, who arranged introductions, explained local practices and politics, and helped with the development of strategy while Mr. Guyer worked with the substantive issues as both an educator and an advocate.

It was my pleasure and privilege to work closely with Mr. Guyer for several years. Bob represented the Portable Rechargeable Battery Association, an international consortium of manufacturers, distributors and users of nickel-cadmium and other rechargeable batteries. My role was as a representative of the Dry

Battery Section of the National Electrical Manufacturers Association, a trade association of United States manufacturers of dry cell batteries. Together we worked with members of state legislatures from Massachusetts to California, and from Minnesota to Florida, on environmental issues concerning the content, disposal and recycling of different types of dry cell batteries. The culmination of the efforts came in 1996 with the enactment of the "Mercury-Containing and Rechargeable Battery Act" (42 USC 14301 et seq.), which codified at the federal level the conclusions which had previously been reached in many of the state legislatures.

Bob leaves two legacies, his success in working with state legislatures across the country and now his work to help others do the same. We are indebted to him on both counts.

Ray Balfour, Vice President
Rayovac Corporation
Madison, Wisconsin
December, 1999

Author's Welcome

Welcome to *Guide to State Legislative Lobbying*. It is likely that you are reading this book because you realize that the state legislature can greatly affect your life and livelihood. Among its many powers, the legislature regulates land use, individual contracts, torts, and business and property transactions. It grants privileges such as licenses to operate a business, practice a profession, drive, and marry. It defines crimes and prescribes punishment. Finally, it takes money from many through taxes and gives it to others through government benefits.

The good news that you will learn from this book is that you have the ability to affect the legislature. This book has been written to lead you systematically through the steps related to successful accomplishment of your legislative goals. Beginning with those activities that prepare you for lobbying – you will identify your problem, assess political strength, develop your lobbying campaign, and perhaps hire a contract lobbyist. Next, you will learn how to negotiate with others and gain support and weaken opposition of special interest groups. After learning the fundamentals of legislative procedure, you will learn to lobby lawmakers to find a main sponsor for your bill and build support among legislators. Finally, you will learn how to interact effectively with the legislature's committees and will learn the steps to take after the legislative session concludes.

Much of the information in this book comes from lobbying in Washington, D.C. and in a number of different states. I have also included my reflections on how lobbying should be done, the experiences of others, and information provided by state legislatures.

Today, the future for state legislative lobbying is exciting! The federal government is returning to the states some of the domestic authority taken during the New Deal. Less and less will Congress solve domestic matters; states will be expected to find their own solutions. Associations will find themselves spending less time in Washington on domestic matters and more time in state houses as helped edit the final drafts and extracted from me what I really wanted to say. Without her unfailing love, infinite patience, and commitment to me, this work never would have been completed.

PART 1

Preparing to Meet the Legislature

1 What is Lobbying?

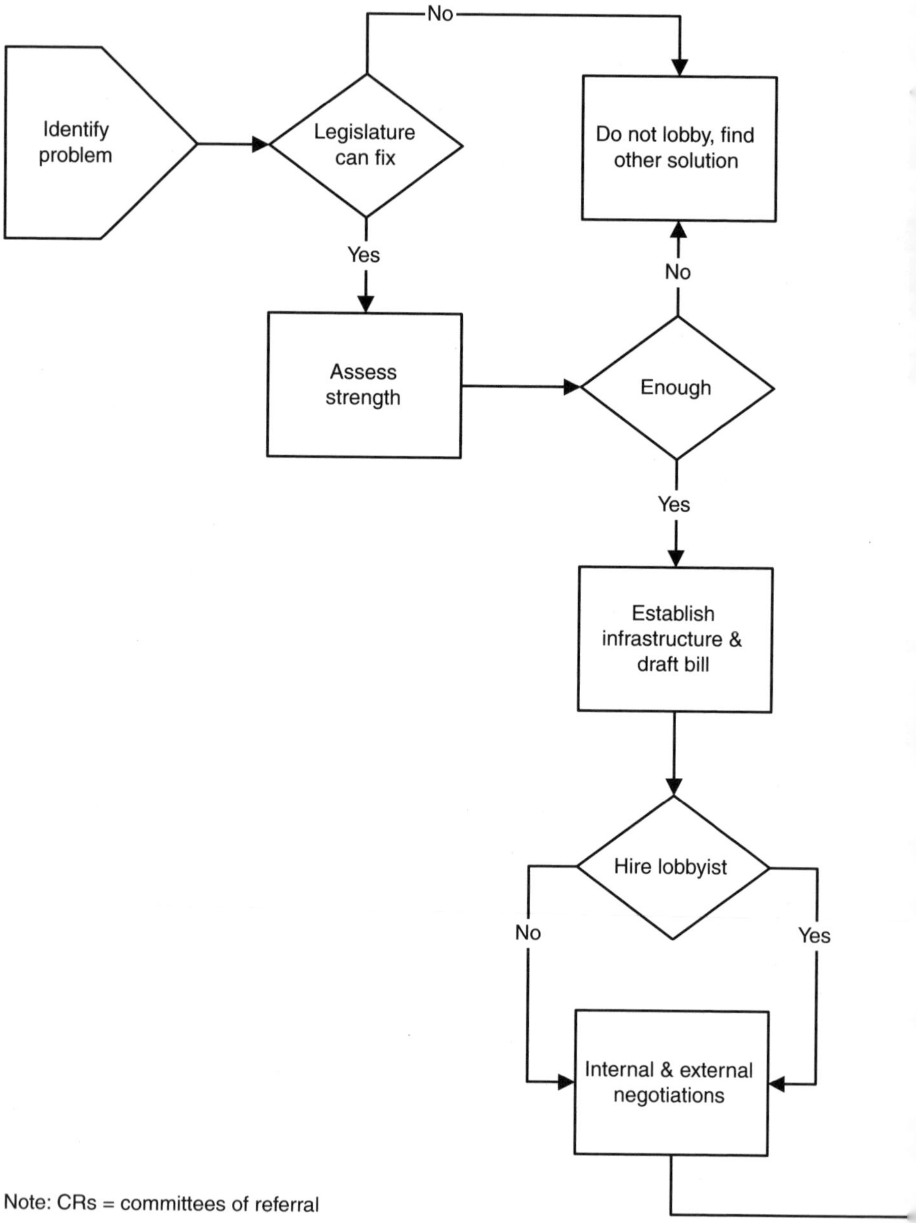

Note: CRs = committees of referral

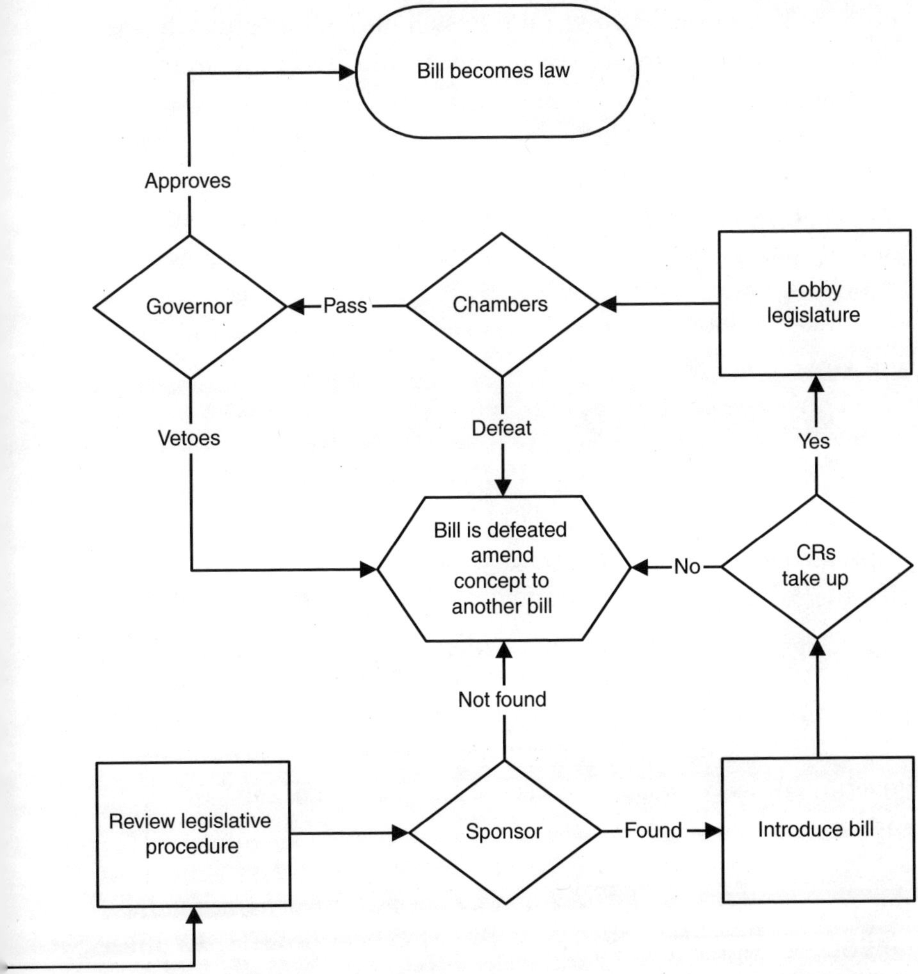
Bill becomes law
Approves
Governor
Pass
Chambers
Lobby legislature
Vetoes
Defeat
Yes
Bill is defeated amend concept to another bill
No
CRs take up
Not found
Review legislative procedure
Sponsor
Found
Introduce bill

Understanding why you can successfully affect the legislative process requires some basic understanding of the United States' form of civil government. Our government is a form of representational democracy called a republic. In every state and at the federal level are three branches of government: the legislative, executive, and judicial. The legislative branch is comprised of representatives from the legislative districts in a state. It "is responsible for translating the public will into public policy for the state, levying taxes, appropriating public funds, and overseeing the administration of state agencies."1 Translating public will into public policy enables legislatures to make laws on any topic, except as limited by state and federal constitutions. The executive branch implements the laws enacted by the legislature and has limited participation in the legislative process. The judicial branch, or court system, evaluates the conduct of individuals relative to laws and has limited review of the actions of the legislature and Governor.

Our representative government in the United States is strikingly different from other democracies worldwide. To many foreigners, the U.S. system that encourages all citizens to participate and is open to citizen and legislator influence appears unpredictable, inefficient, disorderly, aggressive, contentious, and chaotic. Arising from an ingrained distrust of state power and with the belief that government belongs in the hands of the people, the framers of our Constitution sought to establish and maintain the people's control of government by designing a system of open citizen participation. Consequently, people do participate in government as lawmakers, citizens, interest groups, and others to support a range of positions.

As the legislature exercises its authority, it is accountable to the people. Accountability provides opportunity to individuals and groups to influence government. The citizen effort to affect government is called by various terms such as influencing, influence peddling, persuading, petitioning, and most commonly, *lobbying.* Because our system is open to citizen participation and responsible to the citizenry, it is designed to be influenced, that is, it is designed to be lobbied. Simply stated, lobbying is telling your elected representatives about your needs and then motivating them to help you satisfy those needs through the enactment of legislation.

If you have or expect to have some vital interest before the state legislature, you will likely try to influence the outcome of that issue as it is considered. You will then join the ranks of the tens of thousands of others who participate in democracy as lobbyists, U.S. style.

Lobbying and citizen rights

Lobbying, itself, is a simple concept. It is the active expression of a citizen's right to influence government. This underlying right to influence government is so fundamental to a democracy and the United States' system of government that it is guaranteed by the First Amendment to the Constitution, "The Congress shall make no law...abridging...the right of the people peaceably to assemble, and to petition for redress of grievances." Chief Justice Charles Evans Hughes stated, "The maintenance of the opportunity for free political discussions to the end that government may be responsive to the will of the people and that changes may be obtained by lawful means, an opportunity essential to the security of the Republic, is a fundamental principle of our constitutional system."[2] In his 1964 classic, *Lobbying and the Law*, political scholar Edgar Lane wrote, "lobbying is not an American invention." Lobbying has long been one of the means by which citizens can bring their needs to the government. However, "The American experience is unique in the degree to which diverse interests have proliferated and sought political expression. It is unique in the degree that our institutional arrangements were intended to conduce and have conduced to this end."[3]

Lobbyists and lobbying have changed a great deal over the 130 years since the term "lobbyist" was first coined. Lane noted, "The term 'lobbying' has been in common use for more than one hundred years. Throughout the nineteenth century, it meant face-to-face efforts by paid agents to influence legislators to vote in their clients' behalf, often by corrupt or covert means."[4] "Eighty years ago, lobbying meant personal solicitation of legislative votes, usually, but not always through the agency of hired lobbyists, of whom there were relatively few. These men traded on their privileged entree to committees, their specialized knowledge of the legislature's procedural lacunae, their skill as hosts, and not infrequently their adeptness at honest argument. And when all else failed, they were prepared to buy their clients the legislation they needed. Overt corruption was common enough to justify [the] general comment that 'lobbying methods were unscrupulous.'"[5]

Some people still think that lobbying is unseemly because certain tactics of the early lobbyists, such as bribery, were criminal. Distaste arises today when lobbyists are found engaged in controversial activities such as paying for legislators' trips, providing legislators with honoraria for speeches to special interest groups, and using questionable methods to make campaign contributions. However, today's effective lobbyist has moved away from influence peddling and "shady deals" in "smoked filled back rooms" to become a teacher, communicator, negotiator, and motivator.

Lobbying has changed. "The staple work of the representatives of major interests concerned with legislation began to center around detailed, technical craftsmanship in the drafting of bills, the gathering of statistics and descriptive material, collection and analysis of legislation and legislative documents from all over the country, the careful bill-by-bill scrutiny of all that was fed into the legislative hopper session by session, the assembling of briefs on pending proposals and the formal appearance before legislative committees, the preparation and dissemination of large quantities of printed material presenting a point of view for the education of the members of an interest group or for the general public. The conduct of this sort of work required both more professional and more routine skills than the old-style lobbyist possessed."[6]

The influence of those living and working in the district of each elected legislator is the single most powerful force in state lobbying. Today's power lobbying relies on constituents to provide the facts and figures needed to develop sound public policy.

Lobbying in today's United States

Everyone involved with the development of legislation influences its outcome. Generally, the people interested in legislation belong to one of two large groups. The first group consists of members of the legislature and staff and the second is those who either advocate or oppose the proposed legislation. Each of these two large groups has subgroups with their own conflicting and competing goals. And, each lawmaker and lobbyist has his or her own political or personal agenda that influences the position taken on proposed legislation.

"[L]egislatures respond; they seldom lead."[7] Rather than being originators of bills, "legislators work almost exclusively as boards of review to judge proposals brought forward by various groups."[8] Most of the ideas for legislation come from citizen activists, businesses, state agencies, and other persons interested in changing the law.

Today's proposed legislation includes thousands of bills related to hundreds of issues. No legislator can be knowledgeable about all of them and there is never enough time in a legislative session for a lawmaker to become an expert in more than a few matters. Thus, he or she often votes on a number of bills from a myriad of unfamiliar topics.

For this reason, education and strong communication skills are the foundation of effective lobbying. Legislators know that they will be more effective when they learn the pros, cons, and politics surrounding a bill on which they will vote. This is especially true for bills assigned to a committee on which they serve.

Our lawmakers expect that every bill will have supporters and opponents who will present good reasons to support their positions. Therefore, lawmakers listen carefully to both sides of an issue before taking a position. Usually, petitioners *lobby* to secure support from individual legislators and the Governor for their issue. Remember, *lobbying is teaching* legislators about your issue and providing the facts needed to convince them to support your view rather than those of your competitors.

The importance of associations

Each person has a small amount of political power that begins with his or her right to vote. Several other factors including relationships with others, place of residency, party affiliation, wealth, and education add to that initial power. One vote usually makes little difference in an election. One person usually makes little difference when he or she lobbies an entire legislature. However, there is a tool that can be used to multiply the potential of your political power. That tool is to become a member of an association.

An association may be permanent, such as a labor union, or it may be temporary, such as a group united to support or oppose a one-time issue. The members of an association may be individuals, companies, or a coalition of many associations. Without respect to the type of association formed, the goal of all associations is to unite many smaller influences into one stronger political force.

Associations and their members engage in most of today's lobbying. You will find that legislators want to do the most good for the largest number of people. Therefore, they would rather interact with associations that represent many people than with lone individuals. As you venture into the political arena with your issue, you will find many other associations are lobbying their issues. When they learn about your issue, some will support your cause and some will oppose it.

You must decide if you will join with an existing association or form a new one. The formation of a new association can send a strong message to others. A new association, formed to work on a single issue, shows others that there is focus and member commitment to that issue. Often, established and well-known organizations will form a new *ad hoc* association when there is a need for a group on a single issue.

The lobbying principles that will be described in this book have been tested within the context of membership in associations and will be presented from that perspective. To be effective, you must become a member of an association

Differences between state and federal lobbying

The U.S. Congress in Washington, D.C. and each state legislature have different legislative environments that require different lobbying approaches. For several reasons, lobbying in a state is much less resource intensive than federal lobbying.

First, there are fewer members in a state legislature than in Congress, thus there are fewer legislators to search out and lobby. The average state legislature has approximately 140 elected members, of these 40 are Senators and 100 are House members.[9] The state specific numbers of legislators vary considerably and range from Alaska's 20 member Senate, to Nebraska's 49 member unicameral legislature (all called Senators), and New Hampshire's 424 lawmakers, of which 400 are in the House. In contrast, the U.S. Congress has 535 members; 100 Senators and 435 Representatives. These numbers show that there are almost four times as many lawmakers in Congress to be lobbied as there are in the average state capital.

Second, state legislators are much more accessible for lobbying than are members of Congress for two main reasons. First, the state lawmaker is more available because he or she spends more time living at home in his or her district. Second, state lawmakers have fewer constituents to interact with, so you have less competition for his or her limited amount of time. Compare the U.S. Senator from California who has 33,000,000 constituents and lives in Washington, D.C. for most of the year to the California State Senator who lives at home and has 820,000 people in his or her legislative district. The increased accessibility in the state means that you will need fewer resources when lobbying.

Third, state legislators have few or no staff, thus their accessibility to lobbyists and constituents is increased. In contrast, members of Congress have large numbers of personal staff and committees have additional staff. The large size and number of staff often seem to interfere with citizen contact with elected representatives. Thus, more time, money, and other resources are often required to lobby federal legislators.

Fourth, in most states, the legislature is in session for only a few months of the year and legislators know that there is little time to accomplish much. On the other hand, Congress meets in session for the entire year and the two-year full time legislative session, along with other factors, often leads to a sense that the resolution of most issues can wait, and wait, and wait. Resources are saved when an issue is resolved in the state legislature in matter of weeks rather than in the years that Congress often requires.

Fifth, at the state level the pressure on lobbyists to make campaign contributions and the expected size of those contributions is much less than at the federal level. This difference is due to the fact that the costs associated with running a state district campaign are normally far less than for a congressional seat.

Experienced lobbyists know that some techniques that enable successful federal lobbying may not be appropriate for state lobbying. They also know that the lobbying style needed differs from state to state. The successful state lobbyist is one who acquaints himself or herself with the environment of each state legislature in which he or she will work and then utilizes the lobbying style preferred in that state.

Lobbying administrative agencies

The President of the United States and the state Governors have bureaucracies to assist them in the administration of the laws that they, as chief executives, have been elected to carry out. These bureaucracies, called executive or administrative agencies or departments, implement laws to regulate activities such as education, welfare, tax collection, and environmental protection.

Federal and state administrative agencies meet their responsibilities to citizens by promulgating rules and they can be lobbied to affect the rules they make. However, just as federal differs from state legislative lobbying, so agency lobbying differs from legislative.

Administrative agency lobbying is much more technical than legislative lobbying because the purpose of an agency rule is to implement the broad goals of a state statute. By law, the legislature mandates what must be done and then delegates authority to an agency to determine how it is to be done. Like state statutes, agency rules are legally enforceable. For example, the legislature may decree that public health is to be protected from a communicable disease found in fish. The state health agency will then determine how to implement this legislative goal. The outcome may include the promulgation of regulations regarding the water bodies in which to ban or limit fishing, the establishment of allowable concentrations of species of bacteria in lakes, or limits on quantity and quality of discharges of storm water into state waters.

When compared to the legislature, agencies operate under many more legislatively imposed procedural restraints. Although the legislature is governed by certain self-imposed rules of procedure, agency rule making is governed by strict requirements generally found in the state administrative procedures act. A lobbyist must understand the strict procedural limits under which agency rule making operates. These include requirements for notice, conduct of public meetings, citizen comment, and many other procedures.

Lobbyists will find that there are far fewer persons to lobby in an administrative agency than in a state legislature. Unlike the many legislators who come to the state house reflecting the diversity of the state's constituencies, decision making in an agency is conducted by a small number of more homogenous career administrators charged with implementing the legislature's directions. Agency lobbying requires the provision of technical presentations to a small number of agency experts.

As civil servants, agency staff are less susceptible to political pressure than are state legislators who can be voted out of elected office by unhappy constituents. Unlike legislators who face periodic elections, the jobs of civil servants are secure. This enables them to give less attention to the political consequences of their decisions as they focus on the technical issues surrounding the implementation of legislative policy embodied in state statutes.

Summary

Lobbying is influencing lawmakers to enact desired legislation. The U.S. system of representational democracy is designed to be influenced by any association of citizens who desires to participate in the process of legislation. Legislators need information about the thousands of bills on which they must vote and they want to know their constituents' interests.

Lobbying requires investments of time, money, and other resources sufficient to overcome the obstacles that normally exist to legislative enactment. Although the fundamentals of lobbying are the same, the lobbying style used will vary based on federal, state, agency, or legislative environment. Now that you understand that you can influence your elected state representatives, you need to assess your political potential as a player in the legislative arena.

---

1 *Idaho's Citizen Legislature* (1997) at 1

2 Hope Eastman, *Lobbying: A Constitutionally Protected Right,* American Enterprise Institute for Public Policy Research (1977), quoting *Stromberg v. California,* 283 U.S. 359, 369 (1931) at 1

3 Edgar Lane, *Lobbying and the Law*, University of California Press (1964) at 3

4 Id at 4

5 Id at 8

6 Id at 179

7 Jack Davies, *Legislative Law and Process,* West Publishing, Co. (1986) at 4

8 Id at 5

9 The Senate average includes Nebraska's entire 49-member legislature. The House average excludes New Hampshire's 400 House members.

2 Assessing Your Chances of Legislative Success

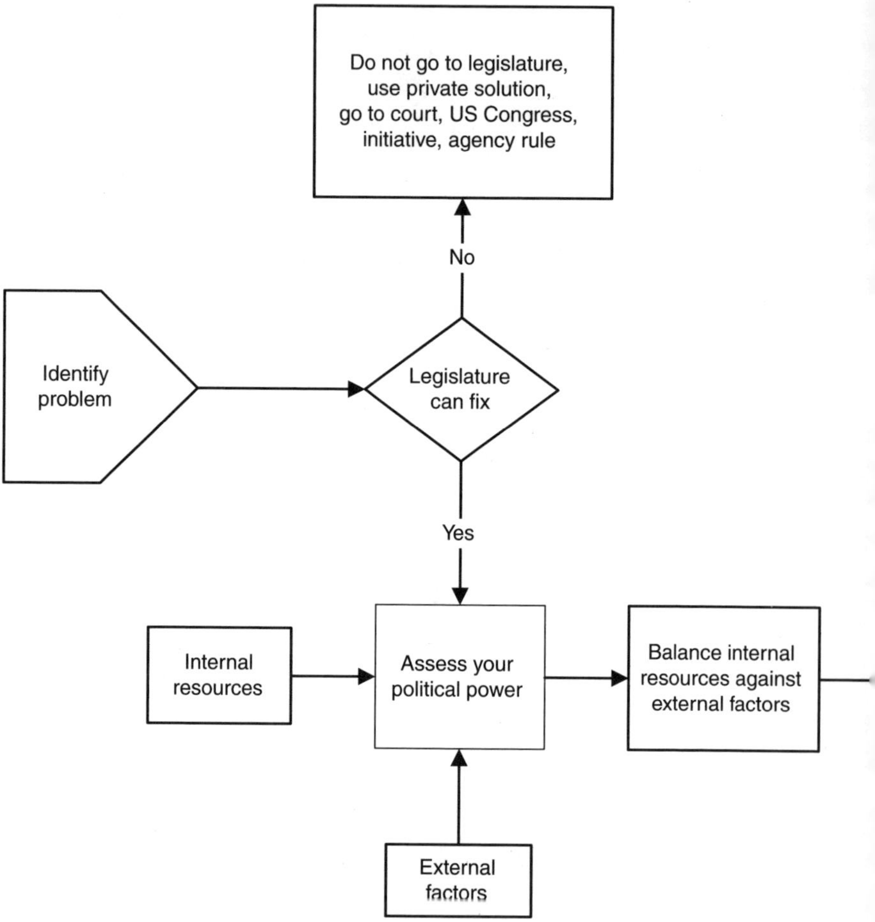

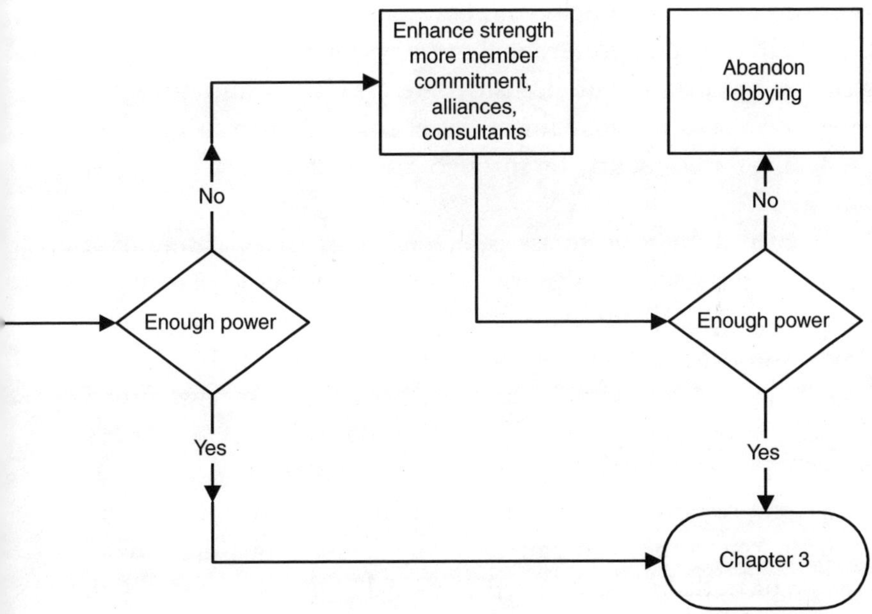
Enhance strength
more member
commitment,
alliances,
consultants
Abandon
lobbying
No
No
Enough power
Enough power
Yes
Yes
Chapter 3

Before embarking on your lobbying project, you should answer four questions. First, "What is my problem?" You must be able to identify and explain your problem clearly so that those who know little about you or your issue can understand it. As you think through your problem, you may find that you have more than one. If this is the case, consider each one separately.

The second question to ask is, "Can my problem be solved without the state legislature?" Some issues, by nature, lie beyond the scope of what the law considers to be appropriate for state intervention. The legislature cannot solve every problem nor is it designed to redress every wrong. Research possible non-legislative solutions to learn whether a private or other public institution might be better able to help you. For example, you may seek certification by a private professional organization rather than ask the legislature to enact a state licensure law. By citizen initiative, you may create a law. You may find a better solution to your problem in federal or state court, or through administrative agency rule making.

The third question to ask is, "Does the state legislature have the legal authority to resolve my issue?" The power of state legislatures is limited by the federal and state constitutions. Further, Congress sometimes takes legislative jurisdiction away from states when it decides to "occupy the field" in an area of law. When Congress occupies the field, it deprives the states of regulatory authority in a particular matter.

Several resources can be used to help you answer the second and third questions. You can begin by contacting professional, industry, or trade organizations that specialize in your issue. Speak to your local legislators, conduct a library or Internet search, contact the administrative agency that would promulgate the required rule, or contact an attorney. You must complete the homework related to your problem before proceeding to the legislature to request the enactment of legislation. By clearly identifying your problem and its possible solutions before entering the lobbying process, you can maximize your expenditures of money, time, relationships, and political capital.

When your research has been completed and if your answers to the first three questions show that you have a clearly defined problem whose solution is best realized through the enactment of state legislation, then you are ready to consider the fourth question, "Will the state legislature solve my problem for me?" The answer to this question will be determined, in large part, by your political strength.

Assessing political strength

Before initiating a lobbying campaign, you must evaluate your political strength. Political strength is defined as the difference between the strength of internal resources and the strength of external factors. You must identify as many internal resources and external factors as possible; then estimate the relative strength or weight of each one. Your political strength must be sufficient to begin the legislative process.

Because a dynamic synergism exists among the internal and external elements, the strength of one can compensate for the weakness of another. Consequently, the presence or absence of a single resource or factor cannot be used to determine the absolute political strength or weakness of an association.

Association internal resources

An association derives its political strength from its members. You can assess the internal strength of your association by considering:

1. Association consensus
2. Member motivation
3. Relationships

4. Places where members live and work
5. Shared characteristics with legislators
6. Membership size
7. Reputation
8. Technical, lobbying, and negotiating skills
9. Ability to form alliances

1. Association consensus

Association consensus is the bedrock upon which to build your legislative effort because it translates into cohesiveness and member motivation. Consensus building for your legislative effort begins when the leaders of each group within the association reach agreement on the nature of the problem and its legislative solution. Then, together they explain the problem, offer the solution to the general membership, and ask for support. Once member support has formed, the association formally adopts goals and a proposed legislative solution and communicates them to the entire membership.

At the conceptualization stage, member consensus usually runs high. As time passes during the process of developing a series of concrete actions to be taken, consensus may weaken. You must work to maintain it, and two of the most effective tools are communication and member involvement.

Those engaged with the legislative effort must maintain on-going and candid communication with the association's members. Early and on-going member awareness of the association's activities will help curtail misunderstanding and disagreement. Communication, for example, will prevent an uninformed association member from contacting his or her legislator to object to something in the bill that the association is lobbying. The resulting confusion from the apparent intra-association conflict would burden the bill with unnecessary controversy and reduce the likelihood of successful enactment.

Member participation in the lobbying effort leads to member "ownership" which builds cohesiveness and maintains consensus. Involve as many members in lobbying activities as possible. Ask less participatory association members to become more involved by writing a letter, visiting a legislator with whom they have a constituent relationship, or accompanying one of your association lobbyists on a lobbying visit.

The consensus that you build must be more than mere member acquiescence to the association's legislative goals. To be useful and productive, consensus must lead to member motivation.

2. Member motivation

Members must be motivated to work for the successful accomplishment of your goals. In permanent associations, motivation to work on a single issue is often more difficult to achieve and maintain because the members have so many other issues to become involved with. On the other hand, in temporary or ad hoc associations that form in response to an immediate and specific concern, members are usually highly motivated and focused to work on the single issue.

Motivation is difficult to measure. However, you can estimate the degree of motivation by testing the willingness of members to use their resources to support the lobbying effort.

Develop a checklist that clearly identifies the types and amounts of resources that members must contribute to implement a successful lobbying campaign. Determine how many and which members should participate in the project. Estimate the time requirements and amount of money that members will need to contribute. Will members encourage other individuals, associations, and legislators that they know to take action on behalf of the association's goals? Once you have completed the checklist, ask your members to commit the necessary resources. Then, determine whether your needs will be met.

Achieving consensus is only the first step in initiating your lobbying effort. Consensus must manifest itself clearly as member motivation. If you find that your members actively support the association's effort, you can proceed to assess the other internal resources. Throughout the lobbying campaign, you will need to nurture consensus and motivation. Once your association reaches consensus and you are satisfied that your members are motivated, you can then evaluate the remaining resources.

3. Relationships

Those who influence legislators most are people who have established positive personal relationships with them. Because they are members of a community, legislators develop relationships with family, friends, acquaintances, neighbors, political allies including fellow legislators and lobbyists, co-workers, clients, employees, members of their places of worship and social clubs, and colleagues in professional societies. Each relationship provides an opportunity to influence a legislator. As you estimate the political strength of your association, carefully determine the number, type, and depth of relationships that each association member has with different legislators.

4. Places where members live and work

A lawmaker's first concern is for the people who live and work in his or her electoral district. Legislators, who hold their offices at the pleasure of their districts' voters, respond attentively to the concerns of their constituents. Thus, they are more inclined to support an association's message when championed by their constituents. You have greater political strength when your members reside in a number of different electoral districts because you have more opportunity to gain support from a number of different legislators.

5. Shared characteristics with legislators

An association member who shares characteristics with a lawmaker can be a more effective lobbyist for that legislator. Shared gender, political party affiliation, political or social views, occupation, and many other characteristics can favorably predispose a legislator toward your association member and, therefore, your issue.

6. Membership size

In general, the larger the number of members in your association the greater its influence. Legislators seek to do the most good for the greatest number of people; thus, they often place the greatest significance on those issues belonging to associations with large memberships. Realizing this, you can increase your political strength by making your association as large as possible.

7. Reputation

Assess your reputation by asking these questions. Do legislators know my association or its members? If known, what opinions do they have about them? Is my association or its members seen as influential or are they unpopular?

The reputation of your members directly affects the power of your association and its political influence. When you attract respected community and organization leaders to your association, their public image and goodwill become associated with your issue and make it more attractive to others.

8. Technical, lobbying, and negotiating skills

Legislators place greater confidence in the statements made by persons with specialized training or experience. When association members have highly specialized, professional, or technical credentials, especially in the subject matter of the proposed legislation, you will have added political strength. For example, a farmer with a master's degree in entomology will be more persuasive than a "weekend gardener" when speaking about the impacts of pesticides on agriculture.

You will have increased political strength if some of your members have previously participated in lobbying or legislative negotiations and have established relationships with legislators or other associations. You should explore how the skills and relationships of your members can be used to advance your issue. Use the negotiating experience of your members to help the association make good decisions and encourage those with lobbying experience to teach the other members to become more effective lobbyists.

9. Ability to form alliances

Your members are likely to hold memberships in other associations. Ascertain their ability and willingness to leverage these relationships to help you build alliances with other associations.

Assessing external factors

Once you have evaluated your internal resources, you must next evaluate the external factors that support and oppose your bill, within and without the legislature. These factors are largely beyond your control and include:

1. How broadly compelling is your issue?
2. How little change you can accept?
3. Identifying potential winners and losers
4. Partisan composition of the legislature
5. The theme of the legislative session
6. The rate of bill passage

1. How broadly compelling is your issue?

Begin your external assessment by estimating the amount of public support that exists for your issue and the amount of support that must be cultivated. Lawmakers often hesitate to support controversial bills or bills that will benefit a few at the expense of many. Therefore, make your bill as non-controversial and widely beneficial to others, as possible. If you can honestly associate your issue with commonly supported causes or beliefs such as children, health, environment, or better jobs, then the goodwill associated with these topics may broaden your support.

2. How little change can you accept?

The less you ask for, the more likely you will get it. But *do not ask for less than you need.* Once the legislature has given your issue attention, they may not want to address it again for several years.

3. Identifying potential winners and losers

Every law has winners and losers. When evaluating external factors, you must determine who might support or oppose you. Besides your association's membership, who will benefit if your bill becomes law? Who will lose? Assess the significance of the impact of the win or the loss on other persons, as this will predict the magnitude of their support or opposition to your proposed legislation. Consider the political risks for each of those who support you. Will supporting your bill, for example, cause a lawmaker to lose the support of other legislators or interest groups for bills that he or she considers important?

4. Partisan makeup of the legislature

The degree of partisanship within each chamber and in the legislature can greatly affect the likelihood of your success. Liberals who lobby a conservative legislature or conservatives who lobby a liberal legislature should know that they face political opposition before they mention their issue.

If your association usually supports one political viewpoint, you must consider the popularity of that view within the current legislature. When you lobby, be aware that the lawmakers of one political philosophy may be more open to your legislative proposal than those with other philosophies.

5. The theme of the legislative session

The legislature and the Governor set goals each legislative session that establish a session's theme. In one session the theme may consume the attention of the legislature, while in another, less attention will be required. The theme is important because it affects the types of proposed legislation that the legislature will favor in a given session. You must discover the legislative session's theme before drafting or lobbying your proposed bill. Legislators and others acquainted with the legislature, especially those in the majority party, can accurately estimate the forthcoming year's theme and its likely effect upon your legislative proposal.

Once you know the theme, ask yourself, "How well does my issue fit within it?" If your issue fits, then the likelihood of enactment is greater than if it does not. If you cannot fit your issue into the session's theme, then you have three choices. The first is to wait for a later, more favorable session. The second is to draft your bill so as to require little legislative time and attention to enact. Small, non-controversial bills may sometimes be enacted even when the session focuses on a different theme. The third choice is to proceed regardless of theme if your bill is necessary this year.

6. The rate of bill passage

Each jurisdiction has a success rate for bill enactment. Some states enact almost fifty percent of introduced bills while others enact less than ten percent. Knowing the bill pass rate in your state will provide a general estimate of your probability of enactment. When you compare the issues in your bill to those that have passed, you will gain even more information about the likelihood of success.

In addition to the success rate in jurisdictions, you should be aware that bill enactment is affected by sponsorship. For example, a member of the minority party in the chamber who sponsors your bill is less likely to be successful than is a member of the majority party. As you consider potential sponsors and lobbyists for your bill, examine their rates of success at bill passage.

Are you a tax-exempt organization?

Tax laws may limit the amount of money that may be spent on a lobbying effort. Federal 501(c)(3) and (c)(4) organizations and state tax law equivalents, as well as organizations that receive government funding, must ensure that their expenditures do not exceed federal and state limits on spending for legislative activity.

Weighing internal resources against external factors

Once the internal resources and external factors have been identified and evaluated, you can estimate your political strength by finding the difference between them. How do your internal resources compare to the external factors? Do you have enough political strength to begin your legislative effort? If not, can you increase it? As you estimate political strength, realize that this is a subjective evaluation that requires your best judgment.

Assessing your internal resources and external factors places you at a crossroads in the lobbying path as you must now decide whether to continue with your project or abandon it. You may find that although your political strength is insufficient, you have little choice but to move forward because of an urgent need for legislation. Ideally, however, you will move forward only if your political strength seems to be sufficient.

Increasing your political strength

If your initial assessment suggests insufficient political strength, you can grow stronger. Although you can do nothing about this year's partisan composition of the legislature, the theme for the session, or your tax status, you can affect some of the internal resources and external factors.

Highly motivated association members that are willing to commit to your legislative success can compensate for deficits in other internal factors. You can also increase the legislators' awareness of your association and its expertise. By joining with other individuals, companies, or associations who have the resources that you lack, you can add to your political strength.

Specialized consultants are available to help you in most areas. Especially valuable are contract lobbyists who are experts in advocating legislation and who have a network of political contacts. You may be able to reduce opposition and gain support by redefining your issue to make it more compelling or by revising your legislative goals to fit better with the session's theme.

Summary

Your assessment of political strength begins with consideration of internal resources and external factors. The dynamic synergism among these variables can enable you to move forward even when some factors are not favorable toward you or your issue.

Political strength is the difference between the power of your internal resources and external factors. It is a subjective evaluation. When you have sufficient political strength, or when you are able to increase it sufficiently, you can proceed to develop the lobbying campaign. In this next step, you will design the association's infrastructure, develop the lobbying plan, and draft your preliminary bill.

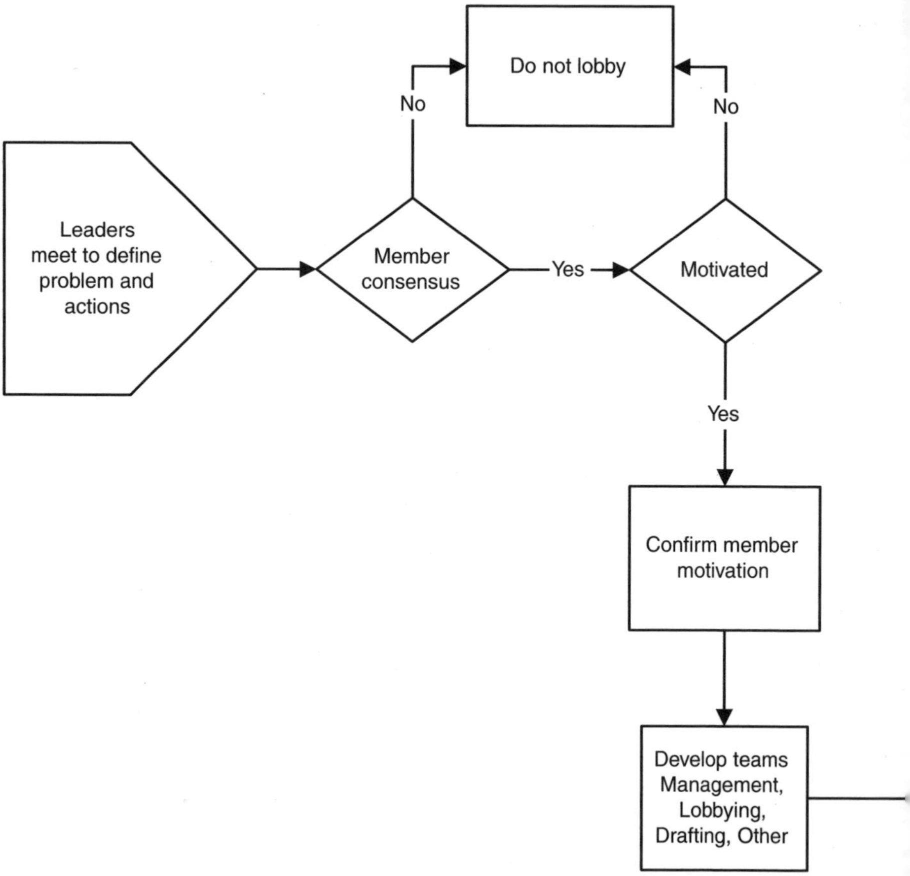
Do not lobby
No
No
Leaders meet to define problem and actions
Member consensus
Yes
Motivated
Yes
Confirm member motivation
Develop teams Management, Lobbying, Drafting, Other

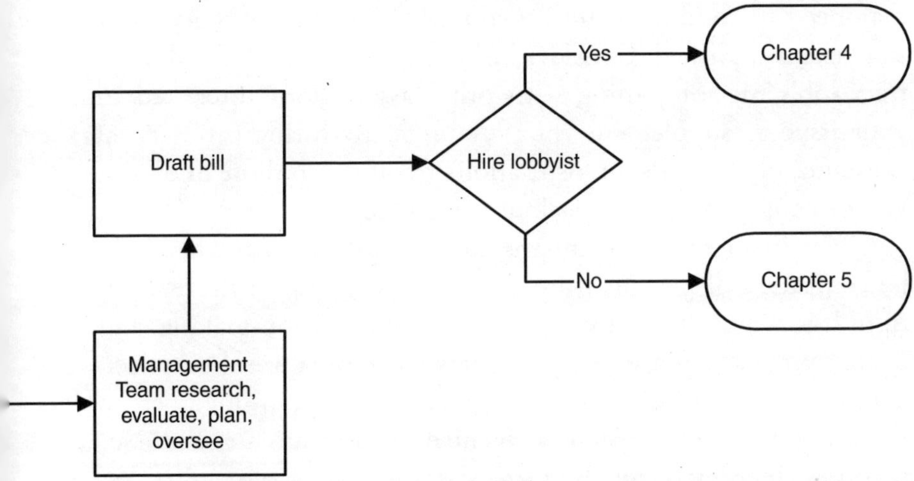
Yes
Chapter 4
Draft bill
Hire lobbyist
No
Chapter 5
Management Team research, evaluate, plan, oversee

Although lobbying itself is a simple concept, its practice involves a systematic progression of activities and decisions. Now that you have sufficient political strength in your association, you will develop the association's infrastructure and strategy to move the lobbying campaign forward. The infrastructure has two broad categories of distinct yet interdependent teams, management and functional, that enable the effective planning, organization, and implementation of your campaign. Once the infrastructure and lobbying plan have been developed, then you can draft your bill.

The infrastructure

Teams form the infrastructure of your lobbying campaign and the size of your association will determine the number of individuals available to serve on each one. If your association is small, you may need to combine team functions so that the necessary work can be accomplished. Consider hiring consultants, law firms, contract lobbyists, or joining with other associations interested in your issue to supplement your resources. By hiring professional assistance or joining your association's resources to those of others, you can compensate for a lack of personnel.

The first team to organize is the *Management Team.* It should be comprised of persons from each interest group in the association. It is responsible for strategic planning, decision-making, and overall project management. This team will organize the project, commit resources, develop project goals, and appoint members to the functional teams. The Management Team translates the association's legislative goals into specific outcomes, allocates resources, and develops a rationale and strategy for the project. Therefore, it should be comprised of politically savvy managers who understand human nature and know how to work with people, especially those with opposing views.

The Management Team must ensure that there is effective communication among the teams' members as the project advances. Even the best campaign will fail if individuals or teams lose sight of the overall goal or become focused only on their personal interests or responsibilities.

One functional team, the *Lobbying Team,* is composed of association members and the contract lobbyist, if any. The Management Team assigns broad legislative goals to this team. They respond by lobbying lawmakers and staff, supporters and opponents face-to-face, attending and testifying in committee hearings, and monitoring the activities of lawmakers, supporters, and opponents throughout the life of the bill.

The *Bill Manager* chairs the Lobbying Team. Appointed by the Management Team, the Bill Manager is responsible for overseeing the day-to-day activities of the lobbying effort. He or she coordinates the grass roots lobbying activities of association members and is the designated contact for the association's contract lobbyist(s). The Bill Manager provides feedback to the Management Team about the bill's progress so that changes can be made in policy or resource allocation, if needed. He or she is also responsible for assuring that the association meets the legislature's ethical requirements.

Another functional team, the *Drafting Team,* writes the bill and supporting information that will be given to the legislature. It should be composed of persons who write clearly and can understand legal requirements. The initial supporting information and committee testimony will be drafted prior to bill introduction and revised, as needed.

The *Bill Historian* is an important member of the Drafting Team. The Historian must be a detail-oriented person who records and is able to explain all actual and proposed changes in bill language following its publication to interest groups and introduction into the legislature. As your bill advances along the legislative path, there will be proposed and actual changes in its language and concepts. The Historian must be able to explain all changes to those who inquire so that you will not appear to be dishonest or incompetent if asked about differences among successive drafts.

Consider adding other functional teams to meet the lobbying needs of your campaign. Some of these include grass roots organizing, negotiations, public relations, media, budget, and other activities specific to your project.

The lobbying plan

The lobbying plan describes how you will gain support and minimize opposition. It helps to maximize the use of your resources to increase the likelihood of success. When you assessed political strength, you considered the difference between internal resources and external factors. As you now develop the lobbying plan, consider these elements:

1. People
2. Costs and benefits
3. Timing
4. Place
5. Campaign contributions
6. Communication with the media
7. Avoiding unnecessary conflicts
8. Maintaining confidentiality

1. People

You must identify those persons who can impact your effort as you design the lobbying plan. These will include prospective sponsors and co-sponsors, members of committees of referral, and your bill's likely supporters and opponents inside and outside of the legislature. As you identify each one, consider why each might support or oppose you based on your relationships and the language and ideas in your bill.

Consider the Governor's likely response to you and your bill. Determine whether your bill fits with his or her legislative theme for the session. The Governor may support or oppose your bill depending upon how it fits with his or her agenda.

Identify the executive agencies that may be lobbied to gain political support for your bill. The legislature and Governor will give considerable attention to the recommendations from experts within these agencies.

Special interest groups may be found as corporations, associations, and local governments. You must predict which interest groups may oppose your bill for substantive or political reasons. Can you satisfy, undo, or work around their opposition? Locate your potential supporters and find ways to actively involve them in supporting your bill. Find ways to strengthen their support and look for nontraditional allies for your issue. Think broadly and creatively when considering alliances with others.

Constituents are critical to success. In each district, identify those who can be mobilized to visit a lawmaker, organize a letter writing campaign, develop a telephone tree, or use other methods to generate contacts with their lawmaker.

2. Costs and benefits

Assess the financial, political, social, and personal costs to your association, the supporters and opponents of your goals, legislators, and others. List the benefits of your legislation and then, compare the benefits to the probable costs to your association and others. Try to identify the amount of lobbying needed to maintain support and estimate the cost and benefit associated with each new alliance. You will want to draft your bill to minimize costs and maximize benefits for all that will be affected should your bill become law. Although "win-win" is an attractive concept, in practice most laws benefit one group more than others.

3. Timing

Often, the success of a legislative effort is dependent upon timing. An ill-timed legislative effort may fail despite a meritorious concept. To help you find the best timing for your effort, answer these questions:

a. Can this legislation wait until next year?
b. Would the legislation advance more readily in another year?
c. Will this year's allies still be in office or otherwise able to support you next year?
d. When should lobbying begin?
e. Is there adequate time to meet critical dates, procedural milestones, and political timelines?
f. Are there other time-related conditions, such as deadlines for making campaign contributions, that must be considered?

4. Place

Before taking your issue to the state legislature, consider where the best or easiest place might be to obtain precedent-setting legislation. It might be in a sister state or in a major political subdivision of the state, such as an important city or county. Investigate the legislation passed in states with precedential value for similarity to your issue. Finally, decide which lawmakers to lobby at home and which in their capital offices.

5. Campaign contributions

Will campaign contributions be part of your lobbying plan? On a member-by-member basis, determine how your support of a legislator's re-election campaign will garner goodwill. If you need the support of legislators with whom your association has no constituent interests, campaign contributions may improve access.

However, legislators have the greatest interest in constituents, especially those who make campaign contributions.

Contributions show a lawmaker that you are a member of his or her "team." If you are a tax-exempt organization, campaign contributions will be limited by law to a specific percent of income or prohibited altogether.

6. Communication with the media

Consider how to use the media to promote your bill. Develop press releases that explain the identity of your association, its members, and its lobbying goals. Select articulate, credentialed, or well-known members of your association to represent you to the media. On the one hand, your issue may suffer from media attention if it brings unwanted interest from opposition groups. On the other hand, favorable attention may help you overcome opposition.

7. Avoiding unnecessary conflicts

The association must ensure that its legislative goals and activities do not unnecessarily conflict with those of its members or allied organizations. Your member companies or organizations often have legislative agendas unrelated to the issue advocated by the association. You must coordinate lobbying efforts to avoid sending conflicting messages to the legislature.

The association should also communicate and coordinate activities with the special interest groups whose issues will follow a similar path through the legislature. These other groups will not compete with you on specific issues, but they will compete for the legislature's very limited amount of time, attention, and state funds.

8. Maintaining confidentiality

Once the Management Team has evaluated your issue and developed the lobbying plan, it should be explained orally to all members of the functional teams. Maintain confidentiality about your plan and do not distribute any written details. Too often, written documents are found in the hands of the wrong people, leading to catastrophic results.

Conducting legislative research

You must discover and utilize available information about the legislative process, individuals and interest groups, government agencies, committees, and legislators who will affect the outcome of your bill. Initially, conducting research may seem to be an intimidating task. However, today's technology has simplified the process and expanded the amount of information available.

You can start your research without leaving home. The names and telephone numbers of your local and state representatives and agencies are listed in the telephone book or may be obtained by contacting Directory Assistance. Your elected state representatives may maintain district offices staffed by employees who can answer your questions on a variety of issues. A legislative aide who manages the day-to-day activities in the office can schedule an appointment with the legislator for you to discuss your topic of interest. Legislative aides with access to state resources and personnel can provide you with valuable insight about the political environment in your state capital.

The local library may provide information about state representatives, state and local agencies, and interest groups. References describing the basics of the political process, such as how a bill becomes law, are available, as are books to help you draft your bill.

Many state government activities are conducted with or through local government. Consequently, local government and agency officials are often well informed about state issues and can provide you with information about current issues as well as possible future legislation.

Your state may publish a state guide. These guides show the geographical areas of each elected official's electoral district in addition to the electronic (e-)mail and mailing addresses, fax and telephone numbers, lists of state agencies and representatives, and districting information that you will need. The Office of the Senate Secretary or House Clerk may publish manuals with current information, biographical data, and other relevant facts about all legislators, their committees, and political activities.

The legislature's legislative services agency is another valuable resource for groups interested in drafting their own legislation and supporting information for presentation to their sponsor. One legislative services agency, known in some states as Legislative Counsel or Bill Drafting Services, ensures that bills are correct as to form and law. Although these offices work primarily with lawmakers and not directly with citizens, they may be willing to refer you to an appropriate drafting manual or model on which to pattern your bill and supporting information.

Finally, the major political parties' local and state offices may provide information about current and prospective candidates, party positions on issues, candidate campaigns, and local opportunities for involvement with the party. These offices are listed in the telephone book with other political groups and state agencies.

Internet research

The Internet is an invaluable source of information for most topics related to lobbying your bill. State legislatures maintain home pages that provide information about individual legislators, list state government directories, describe bill drafting procedures, and provide chamber rules. Home pages offer links to sites related to the state's government and topics range from agencies to personnel matters. During the legislative session, the status of bills, journals, meeting notices, and calendars may be listed.

The information or guidelines for drafting legislation in the proper format can be obtained from web sites in each state. Although sample bills may be downloaded to use as models, you should obtain an official paper copy since electronic versions may not show chamber coding, bill summary, tables, or other necessary information.

One of the best web sites for finding pertinent state information is the Findlaw web site. This site can access information from each individual state's directory and the executive, legislative, and judicial branches of government. It may list e-mail addresses, committee names, memberships, and positions of leadership within the legislative branch of each state.

Cornell University offers a web site that provides political information. Here, you can retrieve federal and state constitutions, state statutes by a variety of topics, pending bills, and directory information for each state. There are also links to sites related to the local and national politics of each state as well as to other topics.

Project Vote-Smart, sponsored by persons along the political continuum, tracks and researches state and federal political activities. From the web site, you can find information about local legislators, biographical information, information about how to contact them, bill tracking information, and a variety of links to state and federal sites. It also provides information about legislators such as financial donations, current issues, candidate positions, voting records, and candidate evaluations by interest groups.

States publish information to help you find groups previously interested in legislative topics similar to yours. You may find lobbyists, organizations for which they lobby, and perhaps financial disclosure information. The information is public record and may be obtained from the lobbyist registration office or, in some states, on the Internet.

Drafting your proposed bill

A *bill* is an idea in written form that is publicly presented to the legislature for enactment. Until it takes concrete form as a bill, it remains just an idea. "No law shall be enacted except by bill" is a common phrase in state constitutions and is the practice in all states.

All bills follow a prescribed procedure when introduced into the legislature. This procedure ensures that the enactment of legislation is orderly, fair, and open to the public eye.

Until it is introduced into the legislature, your bill "belongs" to you. This means that you can add or subtract ideas, change the language, change the purpose or goals, or otherwise alter the existing text. However, once the main sponsor introduces your bill into the legislature, it becomes the "property" of the legislature and you will be less able to affect the changes that follow.

Because your bill's language may change several times before it is introduced, you should not be initially concerned with details of the prescribed form. Your main sponsor and the legislature's Legislative Counsel will ensure that its form is correct before it is introduced. Your initial efforts should be to write a well-analyzed, legally correct, and effective document in the general form of a bill. Duncan L. Kennedy, former Revisor of Statutes for Minnesota, wrote, "Bill drafting must have the accuracy of engineering, for it is law engineering; it must have the detail and consistency of architecture, for it is law architecture."[1]

The Drafting Team writes the association's bill and supporting information using data provided by the Management Team. These data include an assessment of the inadequacy of existing law, the association's legislative goals, and reason for enacting a new law. The political context in which the bill will be written must also be provided and the Team must show how the association's goals fit within those of the legislature's themes for the forthcoming session. Finally, the Management Team must identify the bill's likely supporters and opponents, examine the opponents' arguments, and provide rebuttals to each objection. Once all of this information has been provided, the Drafting Team can begin to work.

Your draft bill will have three components: the title, the enacting or repealing clause, and body.[2] The title and enacting clause are relatively simple and may be written quickly. The title should clearly show the purpose or subject matter of the bill and begin with language such as, "An Act to/concerning/relating to" or "A bill to be entitled."

The enacting clause conveys the intent of the legislature to make the bill state law. It declares, "Be it enacted by the General Assembly" or "Be it enacted by the people of the State of ___." The exact language of the enacting clause is prescribed by each state's constitution.

The body clearly identifies sections to be enacted, repealed, or amended and requires the greatest amount of time to write. If new sections are created, they must be clearly identified as, "New Section" or "Section ___ of the code is created to read" followed by the new language. The repealed sections must be identified as, for example, "Section ___ of the code is hereby repealed."

If writing an amendatory or repealing bill, the affected sections of existing law must be denoted and shown in full within the body of the bill. Amended sections must be identified as, "Section ___ is amended to read as follows..." or similar wording. Amended sections must clearly show changes in language. Although the coding varies among states, additions are usually indicated by underlining, by **bold letters**, or by using all UPPERCASE LETTERS. Deletions are indicated by ~~strikeout~~, [bracketing], *italics*, or other codes.

Before putting pen to paper, the Drafting Team should obtain copies of several previous bills from each chamber of the legislature to use as models for your proposed legislation. If your state posts bills on the Internet, you should still go to the Clerk of the House or Secretary of the Senate to secure paper copies. Unfortunately, the digital format does not always show the complete information and correct appearance of the state's bills.

Throughout the process of engineering the law, the Drafting Team should use these questions, derived largely from Revisor Kennedy, to improve their decision-making and bill drafting.

1. Do existing laws already accomplish some of what you desire?
2. Is it better to amend an existing law or create an entirely new act?
3. Should the bill be drafted as a stand-alone or free-standing bill or should it be drafted to pass as an amendment to another bill?
4. Can you draft the bill to relate to the themes of the forthcoming legislative session?
5. Can you draft the bill to decrease the likelihood of referral to unfriendly committees or too many committees?
6. Once enacted, will this law create conflicts with existing law or produce unintended results?
7. Have the constitutional and statutory limitations and court precedents on legislation been observed?
8. Are the provisions of the bill integrated with existing law?
9. Is the use of words consistent with the language in existing statutes?
10. Are the titles of public officers, agencies, and institutions stated correctly?
11. Does the bill embrace only one subject?
12. Is the title an appropriate expression of the subject of the legislation?
13. Is each distinct part of the bill a separate section?
14. Is the enacting clause in proper form?
15. Are amended sections of existing laws set forth in full?
16. Are all conflicting laws repealed by chapter and verse?
17. Are references to the statutes accurate?

18. Does the bill need an effective date that differs from the date specified by the state constitution?
19. Should provisions within the bill become effective at different times?
20. Is a state appropriation needed to implement the bill?
21. Should the appropriation be placed in this bill or in the annual general appropriations bill?
22. How will funding be continued over time?
23. Will the law be enforceable? How and by whom?
24. Is the style of the bill clear and the language understandable?
25. Can the bill be shortened, simplified, or made more clear?

Draft the bill yourself

As association members work together to draft the bill, association consensus and a bill emerge. Laboring over each word and possible interpretation of the language brings oneness as ideas are translated into specific, meaningful terms. Bill drafting is so central to establishing the cohesiveness of the association that it should not be left in the hands of consultants.

Drafting the supporting information

It is likely that more people in the legislature will read your supporting information than will read your bill. Your bill will be among thousands introduced into the legislature during the session so, unless it is of vital importance to lawmakers, few will read it. Among those who do read it, even fewer will remember what it says.

To help lawmakers recall the important points in your bill, you should provide supporting information that explains why your bill should be enacted, identifies its main points, and provides the rationale for each one. This information should be short, specific, and exceed no more than two pages. Give copies to your bill's main sponsor and co-sponsors. The main sponsor may, in turn, give a copy of the supporting information to the legislature's Legislative Counsel to help them incorporate your ideas into the bill's official draft and summary.

Prepare a model letter and press releases for your sponsors that explain their reasons for supporting the bill. Well-developed, easily understood, and concise supporting information can significantly increase your bill's likelihood of success in the legislature.

Shortly before the legislative session begins, the Drafting Team will prepare the written and oral testimony for you to present at the committee hearing(s) on your bill. The oral testimony will be an abridged version of the written, and both must be presented in the formats established by the committee. Ask the staff of the committee of subject matter jurisdiction for a copy of a well formatted written presentation and inquire about the format and customs for oral testimony.

Summary

Developing a successful a lobbying campaign requires careful organization, research, and planning. Distributing the work among teams gives ownership of activities and optimizes member contributions. Planning enables the project to move forward and provides opportunities for all to give input to the lobbying project. Research ensures that the bill will be comprehensive, without conflict, and legally correct.

With a lobbying plan, draft bill, and supporting information in hand, the Management Team is ready to consider the hiring of a contract lobbyist. If you do not hire a contract lobbyist, then your Lobbying Team can begin to lobby special interest groups that support and oppose you, prospective sponsors, legislators, and the Governor.

1 Duncan L. Kennedy, *Bill Drafting,* (1958) apparently self-published.

2 Legislative Counsel or a similar legislative services agency office adds chamber coding, effective date and explanatory notes. It may also prepare analyses of the bill, an economic impact statement, and other descriptors of likely impact upon the state should the bill become law.

4 Hiring and Working with Contract Lobbyists

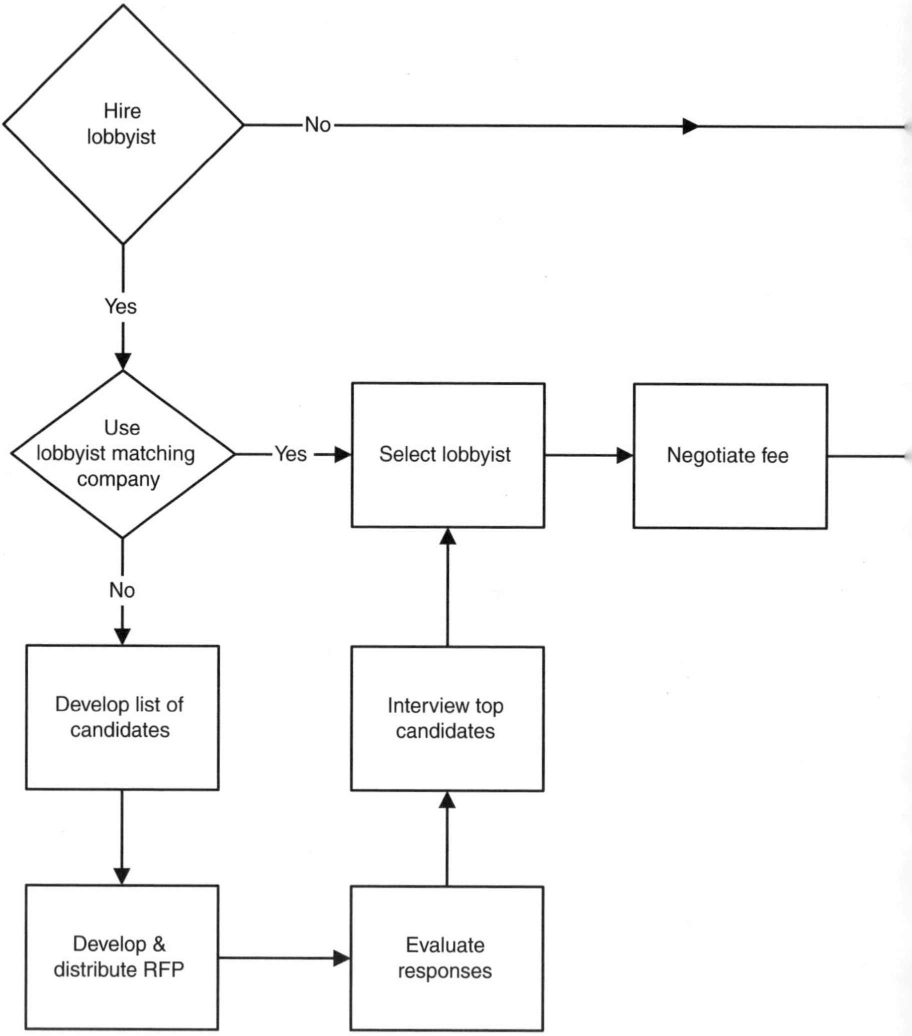

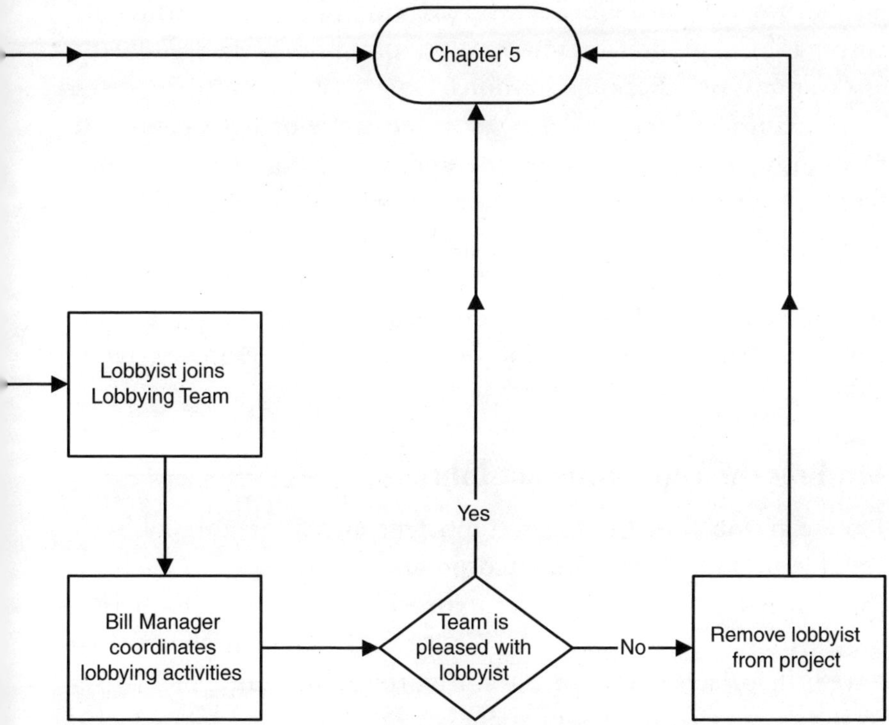
Chapter 5
Lobbyist joins Lobbying Team
Yes
Bill Manager coordinates lobbying activities
Team is pleased with lobbyist
No
Remove lobbyist from project

In your lobbying campaign, one of the most important decisions you will make is whether or not to hire a contract lobbyist. Lobbyists that offer their services on a project-by-project basis may be referred to as "for-fee" or "contract" lobbyists. This distinguishes them from lobbyists who are employees of government, corporations, public interest groups, professional and industry associations, or other organizations.

A contract lobbyist's greatest value is his or her established relationships with persons inside and outside of the legislature who will affect the progress of your bill. He or she will advise you about legislative strategy, tactics, and procedure and will help you maximize your investments of time, money, and other resources in the project. If you decide that you need a contract lobbyist, then you must choose the right one from among the hundreds available.

Finding the right contract lobbyist

How can you find the most competent and affordable lobbyist suitable to your needs? Large corporations and associations have their own legislative affairs departments staffed with lobbyists. When they need to lobby specific issues in states in which they have little presence or need extra help, they hire contract lobbyists in those states. To represent these large corporations and associations, contract lobbyists compete against one another for the business and may reduce their fees or offer other incentives.

When your association is small or is a one-time client with limited funds and offers little hope for future business, some contract lobbyists may not find it cost effective to represent you. Some will not respond to your request for proposal if it asks for too much information and others may not want to be part of your team. Smaller associations should expect that their list of candidate-lobbyists will be drawn from a smaller pool of firms.

Some companies match associations of all sizes to lobbyists that will meet their needs in most U.S. jurisdictions. Stateside Associates and MultiState Associates are companies that can be especially helpful to small associations who expect to have no further issues before the state legislature.

One-time or small clients often have relatively little leverage with lobbyists who, like most contractors, focus their attention on big clients or clients with subsequent or other issues before the legislature. When companies match clients with lobbyists, they help to "level the playing field" because the lobbyist seeks to maintain a good relationship with his or her source of future client referrals.

Since most contract lobbyists do not work through these companies, however, you may want to conduct your own search to consider the full range of available lobbyists for your project. You should develop a list of prospective lobbyists and investigate their interest in securing your association as a client. It is important to manage the screening and hiring process carefully since your candidates will likely tell other lobbyists and lawmakers about you.

Your most effective lobbyist will likely be one who has previously represented interests similar to yours. Ask associations, corporations, and state agencies involved in matters similar to yours to recommend lobbyists based upon their professional experiences. Obtain recommendations from their staff lobbyists. Annually, your state publishes its lobbyist registry that lists all state-registered lobbyists, their clients, and sometimes their fees. You can obtain a copy from the Internet or state office that publishes the registry, often this is the ethics office, House Clerk, Senate Secretary, or Secretary of State.

Lobbyists to exclude from consideration

Some lobbyists should be excluded from consideration as you develop your list of candidates. Avoid any lobbyist who is an employee or contract lobbyist of one of your association's members. If you hire a lobbyist employed by an association member, a situation may later arise that would force the lobbyist to choose between the interests of the association member and you. In a conflict, the lobbyist could choose the member over you and abandon the association or overtly or subtly undermine its efforts.

Further, in an association comprised of members who are competitors, group cohesiveness may be undermined by a suspicion that the lobbyist is loyal only to the member-employer. The other members of the association may fear that their competitor's lobbyist will use association representation as an opportunity to advance their employer's interests at the expense of other members.

Do not ask a legislator to recommend or evaluate a lobbyist and delicately rebuff any unsolicited recommendations. Some lawmakers will recommend certain lobbyists in order to accrue or pay back their political debts. If you receive a recommendation but do not hire the lobbyist, you may cause the legislator to resent you, your issue, and the contract lobbyist you do select. The legislator may be upset by the perceived loss of political benefit or may be annoyed that you wasted his or her time getting advice that was ignored. The lawmaker may also be embarrassed if he or she informs the lobbyist about making a recommendation and you do not follow through with interest or an offer.

Be cautious when considering former Governors, Senate Presidents, House Speakers, and other leaders of high offices as lobbyists. Those who have held the highest offices may be less willing or able to appeal to former opponents or less important legislators for support. This is especially true when they lobby members of the opposing party. Former leaders may have made political enemies when they assigned offices, parking spaces, and staff. There may also be lingering resentments over their choices for committee chairs, assignments of bills to committees, and other uses of power. And, former leaders who have grown comfortable with issuing orders to others, may now find it difficult to follow your orders and may be very difficult to work with. The most suitable lawmaker turned lobbyist is usually drawn from the rank-and-file legislators and staff.

These scenarios are not absolutes. The employees of members have served associations well, lawmakers have made excellent suggestions about prospective lobbyists to hire, lobbying efforts have not been damaged when a recommended lobbyist was not hired, and former leaders have been effective. The consequence of hiring the wrong lobbyist, however, is potentially disastrous. Because there are many lobbyists available, avoid taking unnecessary risks.

Steps to engaging a lobbyist

The Management Team or Lobbying Team should begin the search for your lobbyist at least six months before the legislative session starts, and complete it within three months. This time frame provides an adequate amount of time to find your lobbyist, incorporate him or her into your strategic plan, and begin the pre-session lobbying of lawmakers.

Once you have completed the list of acceptable candidates, you will send a request for proposals (RFP) to each one. The recruitment and selection of candidates consists of five steps:

1. Developing and sending the RFP
2. Evaluating the responses of prospective lobbyists
3. Conducting personal interviews with the most acceptable candidates
4. Selecting the best candidate
5. Negotiating the terms and fees of the agreement

1. Developing the RFP

Your RFP must be complete, specific, well-written, and should:

a. Provide a description of the association that identifies its name, purpose, and a list of members and association staff.
b. Name other lobbying coalitions or groups to which the association belongs.
c. Explain what you want the lobbyist to do: provide general legislative representation without a specific goal or lobby for specific goals this session.
d. Clearly state your lobbying goals and identify what you want the legislature to do. Do you want it to enact or defeat a bill?
e. Clearly identify the role of your lobbyist in implementing your strategy. Identify the association's committees that will work with the lobbyist. It is very important to begin the lobbying relationship with a clear understanding of how he or she will work with your Management Team, Lobbying Team, and Bill Manager.
f. Ask for a description of the expected theme(s) of the upcoming legislative session.
g. Ask for a description of how he or she would accomplish your goals and estimate the likelihood of success.
h. Ask for a written statement that verifies no potential conflicts of interest with other clients because of representing you. By reviewing the state's lobbyist registry, you may find the names of the lobbyist's recent clients and potential conflicts.
i. Ask the lobbyist what he or she does when the legislature is not in session. This will give you greater insight as to potential conflicts not gleaned from the lobbyists' registry.
j. Ask for a description of his or her experience in state government. Was he or she ever a legislator? If yes, which electoral district was represented and for what period of time? If the

lobbyist was a staff member, state agency official, or worked for the legislature, ask for whom he or she worked, a description of the position, and for the number of years served.

k. Ask how long he or she has been lobbying and determine if he or she has ever lobbied an issue similar to yours. If yes, what was the result?
l. Ask the candidate if he or she has appeared before the committees that have jurisdiction over the subject matter of your issue. If yes, for which clients and for what issues?
m. Ask for a description of his or her relationships with the chamber leaders of both parties and chairs and members of committees of referral.
n. Ask the candidate to identify those legislators that he or she has supported in their election campaigns. Identify the lawmakers' bills that he or she supported,[1] opposed, or stopped. The candidate's responses will enable you to identify the contacts and political relationships that might be leveraged in your favor or that exist to your detriment.
o. Ask the candidate to explain his or her perception of the existing degree of partisanship in the legislature. The candidate's political party affiliation may be important, especially if the legislature is highly partisan. When all other factors are equal, a lobbyist with the same party affiliation as the majority in the chamber is the better choice. Larger lobbying firms can provide lobbyists who are registered and active in each political party.
p. Ask for a description of his or her lobbying practice and firm. Ask about the issues that the firm has lobbied, the issues they will lobby for in the impending legislative session, and ask for a list of recent clients.
q. Ask who will represent you in the day-to-day activities and ask for the name and credentials of the members of the firm

that can be called upon, as needed.

r. Ask for the names and experience of associates in his or her firm who may also lobby for your bill. Determine how the work will be apportioned among junior and senior lobbyists and ask yourself if you are comfortable with assigning your project to associates.

s. Ask the candidate to estimate the amount of time that will be devoted to lobbying your issue.

t. Ask for an estimate of time demands that other clients and issues will make on his or her availability to you.

u. Ask candidates to list their rates and costs to represent you. Some lobbyists will want to bill per hour while others charge a fixed fee for a project.

v. Clearly state how long you want the lobbyist to work for you. Generally, this will be for one year or for the legislative session.

w. Describe other legislative items important to your members or you.

x. Provide the date when the proposal will be due.

y. List your Bill Manager's name, telephone number, and address as the contact person for the association.

2. Evaluation of candidates

Carefully evaluate the responses to your RFP and rank your candidates based upon an item by item review of their answers to the questions above. Based upon the responses to your RFP, identify those that you think you will be able to afford financially. Later, you will negotiate a final fee.

Select the top two or three respondents for personal interviews. Contact each candidate you will interview to establish a time and place for the meeting. Send a letter of appreciation to all who responded to your RFP to thank them for their time and effort.

Be sure to look at each lobbyist's list of clients to see if there appears to be any conflicts with your interests. Contact the current and previous clients.[2] Ask those who have employed each candidate to describe their experience and satisfaction with the lobbyist's work. Ask what the lobbyist did for them and ask them to be specific. Determine how the lobbying project was managed; did they direct the lobbyist and, if so, how well did he or she accept direction?

3. Conducting personal interviews

The personal interview provides you with an opportunity to evaluate each candidate's appearance, personality, and communication skills. It enables you to determine whether you and the candidate are a good match. Prepare for your meeting with each candidate by again reviewing his or her response to your RFP in detail and formulate questions.

You should designate one person in your group to lead the interview. He or she will be responsible for pacing it, maintaining order, and assuring that all of your questions are answered. In the personal interview,

a. Ask each candidate to describe his or her understanding of your issue.
b. Ask the candidate for further clarification of vague or incomplete responses to the RFP.
c. Evaluate his or her apparent credibility and honesty.
d. Determine the interest he or she has in representing you.
e. Ask about fees.

It is not uncommon to "puff" relationships and accomplishments in an interview. Be skeptical of the contract lobbyist who claims to be every legislator's best friend. Depending upon the political moment, lobbyists have different degrees of influence. Remember that some contract lobbyists are closer to one political party than to the other, some work better on one issue than another, and some work more effectively in one chamber than in the other. Finally, few bills become law solely from the work of one lobbyist. Beware of the lobbyist who claims too much.

4. Selecting the best candidate

After all of the interviews have been completed, you should thoroughly discuss, compare, and rank each candidate. Select the person who seems to best fit your needs.

Do not require your lobbyist to "look" like you. Organizations whose cultures demand uniformity are sometimes tempted to favor lobbyists who "look like them." In some states and for some issues, it can be a liability for the lobbyist to reflect the image of the client to lawmakers. Remember that your lobbyist should be acceptable to the legislators they hope to influence.

5. Negotiating fees

Once you have ranked the lobbyists in order of desirability, you must negotiate a fee. The fees charged by contract lobbyists vary and range from a few thousand dollars to tens of thousands of dollars per legislative session. The amount a lobbyist will charge for services depends on:

a. State being lobbied
b. Single issue or general representation
c. Availability of lobbyists
d. Competition among lobbyists
e. Size and reputation of the lobbying firm
f. Difficulty of lobbying the issue
g. The fit of your issue within the themes of the legislative session

h. The expected amount of work to be done
i. Your value as a client to the lobbyist

States require lobbyists to report the names of their clients and the fees charged. These public records, available from the state agency that regulates lobbyists, can be used to obtain benchmarks for establishing appropriate fees. Keep in mind that the published fees do not necessarily distinguish between lobbying for a single issue and providing general representation.

When lobbyists are widely available and there is competition among them for clients, the fees will be less. In a very busy session, there may be a greater demand for lobbying services than in a less active session. Greater demand translates to higher fees.

Sometimes, large companies or associations will pay a retainer to most of the lobbyists in the capital when they have a very important issue. Their goal is to make lobbyists unavailable to others interested in lobbying the same issue by creating a conflict of interest. Their action reduces the availability of lobbyists and drives fees higher for those who remain.

Larger and more prestigious lobbying firms charge higher fees than smaller firms. Their larger and more prestigious clients are willing to pay more money for these firms to represent them. Unless you are a large organization, do not use these large firms or their rates to establish your benchmarks.

If your issue seems simple or if there is little work associated with it, it will cost less to lobby than one that is difficult. If it fits within the theme of the session, it also will be easier and less costly to lobby.

Finally, a lobbyist may reduce the fees charged to the association if he or she perceives that members of the association may become future clients. You can leverage possible future business opportunities with members as an incentive to reduce a prospective lobbyist's rates. Remember, a lobbyist's fees are always negotiable.

Methods of payment

A "lump sum" or "fixed cost" contract provides incentive for a lobbyist to finish the work in a timely manner. Using this method of payment, the lobbyist works on your project for a predetermined fee, regardless of the amount of time or resources needed to complete it. A fixed fee contract is a gamble for the lobbyist who may suffer a financial loss if your task requires more time or resources than expected. However, he or she may also realize a good profit if the work is completed quickly. For the client, the fixed fee is "safe" because all costs are established in advance of the project.

The lobbyist's preferred method of payment may be dollar per hour, per day, or per week. In this fee arrangement, your lobbyist receives payment for the amount of time spent working on a project rather than for accomplishments. Avoid this method of payment because it is difficult to contain costs and stay within a budget.

Be aware that additional work completed outside of the scope of the contract may incur additional charges. If your lobbyist offers services that extend beyond the contract, ask if there will be additional charges and ask for the amount that will be charged. You should provide a reasonable budget for expenses such as calls, business meals, and photocopying.

Do not offer your lobbyist more than eighty percent of the total amount you have budgeted for lobbying services. Always keep some money in reserve to accommodate the unexpected. For example, you may need to hire an additional lobbyist because of an unforeseen situation with a legislator.

Sometimes, the amount of work required to move a bill exceeds all reasonable and foreseeable expectations. If you have a fixed fee contract, then the entire overage of the project will fall upon your lobbyist. You may want to help offset the financial losses that he or she is absorbing by providing additional compensation.

Expect some lobbyists to ask you for a retainer. This is the payment of an established amount of money to ensure that the lobbyist will be available to you for a specified number of hours each month. A retainer, however, may also require that you pay your lobbyist even if there is no work completed on your issue. Lobbyists may ask specifically for a retainer to monitor legislative activity, but this is an unnecessary expense. Lobbyists who know your interests will always watch for issues that can lead to more of your business. Unless you have specific monthly activities for your lobbyist to complete, avoid retainers.

Lobbyists are hired to give their best efforts. Never suggest that a bonus or additional payment is tied to successful lobbying of your issue. In some states, this is illegal.

Engaging the lobbyist

Although some associations may insist upon a formal contract, a simple letter of engagement will suffice when hiring a lobbyist. Your letter of engagement should clearly state the goals of your project, project duration, duties to be completed, fees, schedule of payment, causes for termination, and requirements for the reporting of activities. Your letter should name the lobbyist who will complete the work and provide the name of your Bill Manager who will serve as the lobbyist's contact with the association.

Working with your lobbyist

Once you have hired your lobbyist, you should never forget that:

1. No one understands or cares about your issue as much as you do.
2. No one can explain the details of your issue as well as you can.
3. Lawmakers want to hear from their constituents much more

than they want to hear from contract lobbyists.
4. You must mange your lobbying effort.

Few lobbyists will be able to convey the technical details of your concerns to others. Few will be able to answer questions as well as you or convey your passion about the need for your legislation.

Although he or she is part of your Lobbying Team, your lobbyist has business interests that differ from and sometimes compete with yours. He or she will act first to protect his or her own long-term interests and well-being. Activity pursued on your behalf will be balanced against the contract lobbyist's own interests and those of other clients. Since the value of a lobbyist is relationships built with legislators, few will risk a reduction of their influence with a friendly lawmaker to advance the interests of a client, especially a client not likely to need their services again.

Even the best contract lobbyist relationship with a legislator is no match for strong expressions of constituent involvement and presentation of factual data related to an issue. This is because you alone understand and must live with the impact of your issue.

Never allow the contract lobbyist to manage your legislative effort. Although he or she is a valuable resource, only the client is able to make certain critical decisions. When a contract lobbyist controls the legislative activities of the client, or when he or she acts without direction from the client, the client's interests are unavoidably compromised.

Further, most lobbyists do not want to be responsible for the major decisions that you should be making. If you, by default or intent, burden your lobbyist with making your decisions, you will force him or her into an impossible position that may result in paralysis or obtaining a bill that you do not want. Only you know what you can accept.

A few lobbyists will not want you to be involved in making decisions, and once the lobbying task has been assigned and fees have been established, they want to be left alone to lobby the bill. They may try to control the lobbyist-client relationship because they see themselves as the experts and you as the novices. They do not want to be "distracted" by contact with novice clients, nor will they accept supervision. Do not work with a lobbyist who will not become part of your overall plan and team. Avoid any lobbyist who would be willing to make your major decisions for you. Listen carefully to the advice that your lobbyist provides to help you navigate through the legislative process but remember that you, the client, must be the final decision-maker.

While remaining in control of your overall lobbying effort, aim for a minimum of direction over the contract lobbyist. Do not *micromanage* your lobbyist. Contract lobbyists are professionals hired for their legislative expertise and political relationships, and they must be free to use their talents to implement the goals that you assign. Micromanagement will frustrate you and your lobbyist. Once your lobbyist demonstrates that he or she is part of your Lobbying Team, your relationship should be one of partnership rather than supervision.

Evaluating performance

You should evaluate the performance of your contract lobbyist at regular intervals. To help you do so, ask him or her to keep a log of activities completed on your behalf. Your lobbyist should provide weekly reports of progress in the early days of the session and in the last hours, reports may be delivered daily or hourly. These reports, oral or written, should describe the activities completed and progress made on your behalf, and should provide updates about your bill's progress. As you evaluate your lobbyist's performance, consider these questions:

1. Does the lobbyist contact your Bill Manager sufficiently in advance so you can plan for and attend critical meetings?

2. Does the lobbyist refrain from making decisions until you have been contacted?
3. Are you included in all major deliberations among the lobbyist, legislators, and staff related to your issue?
4. Has the lobbyist arranged meetings with relevant legislators and committee members? Check the relevance of each legislator prior to meeting with him or her.
5. Has your lobbyist helped to mitigate the effects of the opposition or have opponents of your bill gained strength?

Following the legislative session, your lobbyist should provide a detailed written report and analysis of the effort. This report should describe the successes and failures, likely administrative agency actions to follow, and expectations for the next legislative session.

You will measure the performance of your lobbyist by comparing your goals in the lobbying plan against the results achieved. The simplest and most meaningful measure of overall success is achieving the desired legislative outcome. However, if your bill was not enacted in one legislative session, this does not mean that you and your lobbyist have failed. You may have created momentum that will make enactment more likely in the next session. It often takes three or more years to enact new legislation.

Replacing your lobbyist

Sometimes a contract lobbyist may not meet your needs and you may need to terminate the relationship. Termination prior to the end of the session, however, is a drastic step that should be avoided as much as possible. If you must terminate your lobbyist during the session, relieve him or her of duties and do it without letting anyone external to your association know about it.

If you secured your lobbyist through a firm that matches lobbyists to clients, contact it before taking action. Because they want to satisfy their clients, they may be able to motivate the lobbyist to serve you better.

If you change your lobbyist in mid-session, you may create the appearance of instability on your part and lose the momentum that your bill has gained. Further, an angry lobbyist can damage you and the success of your proposed legislation. He or she might tell others that the termination of your relationship was due to your dishonesty, instability, or insincerity. If your reputation is damaged, it may be more difficult to find another lobbyist to work for you and the legislature may also believe that you are dishonest and untrustworthy. These factors will greatly reduce your chances of legislative success.

The best approach to terminating services is to simply continue working together for the remainder of the contract period; then do not renew the relationship for next year. Negotiate a mutually satisfactory public explanation for not renewing the relationship. As possible, only communicate positive messages about your former lobbyist. Unless he or she has been involved in some scandal involving you, do not disparage him or her. Disparagement discredits not only your former lobbyist, but by association, you and your issue.

Legislative ethics

As you move through the lobbying process, you will confront the need to make consistent ethical decisions in accord with state requirements as well as your own sense of right and wrong. State ethics requirements are designed to make the legislative process as fair as possible by limiting the influences on legislation from factors external to the legislature that are unrelated to the people's business.

Legislators, legislative staff, and lobbyists are subject to ethical standards. The state standards are found in state statutes which have the force of law, in chamber rules that can carry formal and informal sanctions, and in custom which carries informal sanctions.

Although there is consensus about the nature of certain unethical behaviors, a state may have its own unique ethical requirements. Therefore, state-specific statutes and ethics rules should be studied prior to contacting legislators. For example, the lawmakers' practice of "I'll support your bill if you support mine" may be ethical in one state but unethical in another.

Lawmakers must disclose all unique personal benefits from proposed legislation before they take legislative action. Following this disclosure, they may or may not be legally prohibited from voting on a bill. Lawmakers may request to be excused from voting on an issue if there is a conflict of interest. If a legislator is unsure about a possible conflict, the legislative chamber provides lawyers to help members decide if they have an extraordinary personal interest in a bill or a conflict with the public good.

Lobbyist-specific ethics

State ethics requirements seek to limit the influence of the lobbyist to the merits of proposed legislation. This is accomplished by imposing legal limits on the campaign contributions, gifts, honoraria, and similar favors that may be given to legislators and staff. It is enforced by mandatory reporting and carries sanctions for violation.

Although the ethics requirements vary from state to state, your adherence to the following should enable compliance with the ethics requirements of most states.

1. Register if you are close to the statutory "trigger points" for mandatory lobbyist registration.
2. Maintain careful records of your lobbying activities to ensure that you meet the requirements for reporting.

3. File your state-required reports on time and make sure that they are accurate.
4. Make no gifts or contributions to lawmakers or staff during the legislative session.
5. Ensure that all information given to the legislature by you and your contract lobbyist is correct.

Lobbyists are required by law to register with the state office of lobbyist regulation, usually based on the number of contacts with lawmakers. Your contract lobbyist must register. It is likely that your Bill Manager and one or more of your company or association representatives also will be required to register as lobbyists. Because lobbyist registration requirements do not apply to the citizen who has periodic, infrequent contact with the legislature over a single bill, association members who accompany your lobbyist to visit a legislator would not have to register. However, once an advocate becomes a registered lobbyist and makes the legislature aware of his or her existence, then the rules that apply to the reporting, gift giving, and influencing of the legislature are enforced, sometimes vigorously.

Keep a daily record of your lobbying activities and make sure to file periodic reports by their due dates since late reports become easy targets for enforcement. The states differ in their requirements for reporting information. Usually, reports ask for the names of those represented by the lobbyist and the money received, but some states ask for more information. Wisconsin, for example, requires lobbyists to submit a log of the time they spend working on each issue.

Gift giving to lawmakers is not a recommended practice, but if you consider doing it, make sure that you know the state's rules that govern gift giving. In some states, unacceptable personal enrichment includes receipt of campaign contributions, gifts of nominal value, food, and entertainment while the receipt of such things may be perfectly acceptable in other states.

Do not give unique gifts to select legislators. The distribution of low cost "token" reminders of your bill to all lawmakers is generally acceptable, but if you give gifts, give only as clearly allowed by the state's rules. To meet gift giving rules, use the highest dollar value for your gift when estimating its worth. Then make sure that the estimated value is less than the gift giving limit. In some states, lobbyists may be required to identify the lawmakers and staff to whom they have given gifts. They may also need to report the value of those gifts if valued above some threshold amount.

If making campaign contributions, do so before the legislative session begins and after it ends. Some states prohibit contributions during the session.

A lobbyist must ensure that, to the best of his or her ability, the information presented to the legislature is correct. There is an expectation that lobbyists will always be truthful with lawmakers, and a violation of this trust leads to formal or informal penalties. If you inadvertently provide incorrect information, correct it as soon as possible.

Your Bill Manager is responsible for ensuring that the association and its lobbyists comply with state-specific and general rules of ethics. He or she ensures that an ethics violation does not undermine the effectiveness of the association or the lobbying project.

In addition to mandated ethics, you should abide by principles embodied in moral ideals, religion, and social teachings to establish and preserve your reputation for principle, integrity, and honesty. A reputation for principle enables lawmakers and others to predict your response to legislative proposals. Integrity communicates to others that you will follow through on your commitments. A reputation for honesty makes your information believable so that others will not need to investigate your facts any further. A reputation for being unprincipled, unreliable, or disingenuous will destroy your effectiveness as a lobbyist, harm your bill, and can end your career.

Summary

Your employment of a contract lobbyist can help you build beneficial momentum to move your issue forward. A contract lobbyist is a professional with established relationships that can be used to draw the attention of lawmakers to your issue. Your lobbyist will assist you throughout the legislative process. At every step of the lobbying campaign, you must abide by commonly held and state-specified ethical requirements that provide safeguards against potential conflicts of interest or impropriety.

At this point in the process you have established your legislative goals, developed the lobbying campaign, drafted your bill, and made the decision about hiring a contract lobbyist. As you prepare to meet the legislature, the next step will be approaching other interest groups to gain support for your issue or minimize opposition. To do this effectively, you will rely on negotiation skills.

---

1 In politics, the concept that "one good turn deserves another," or the American concept of reciprocity, has built a system in which an act on behalf of someone else builds or discharges a political debt.

2 However, sometimes it becomes necessary "to read between the lines" to learn unpleasant or unflattering information.

5 Negotiation

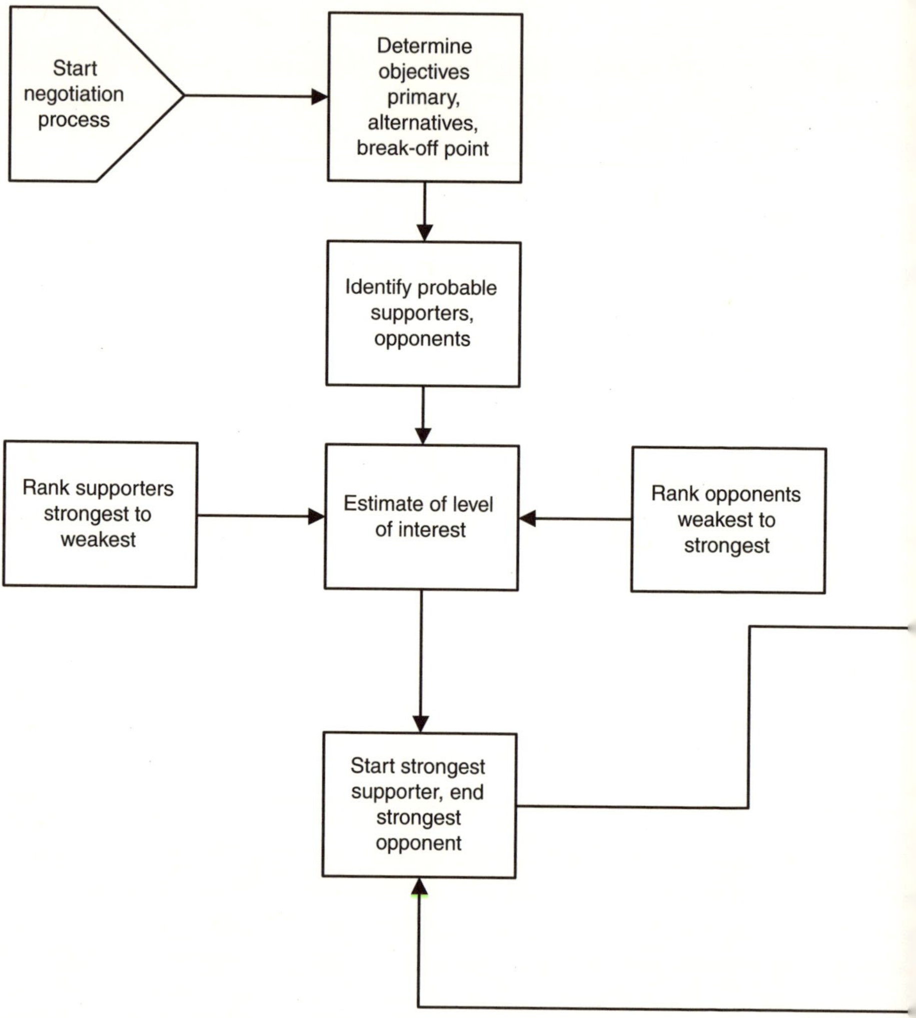

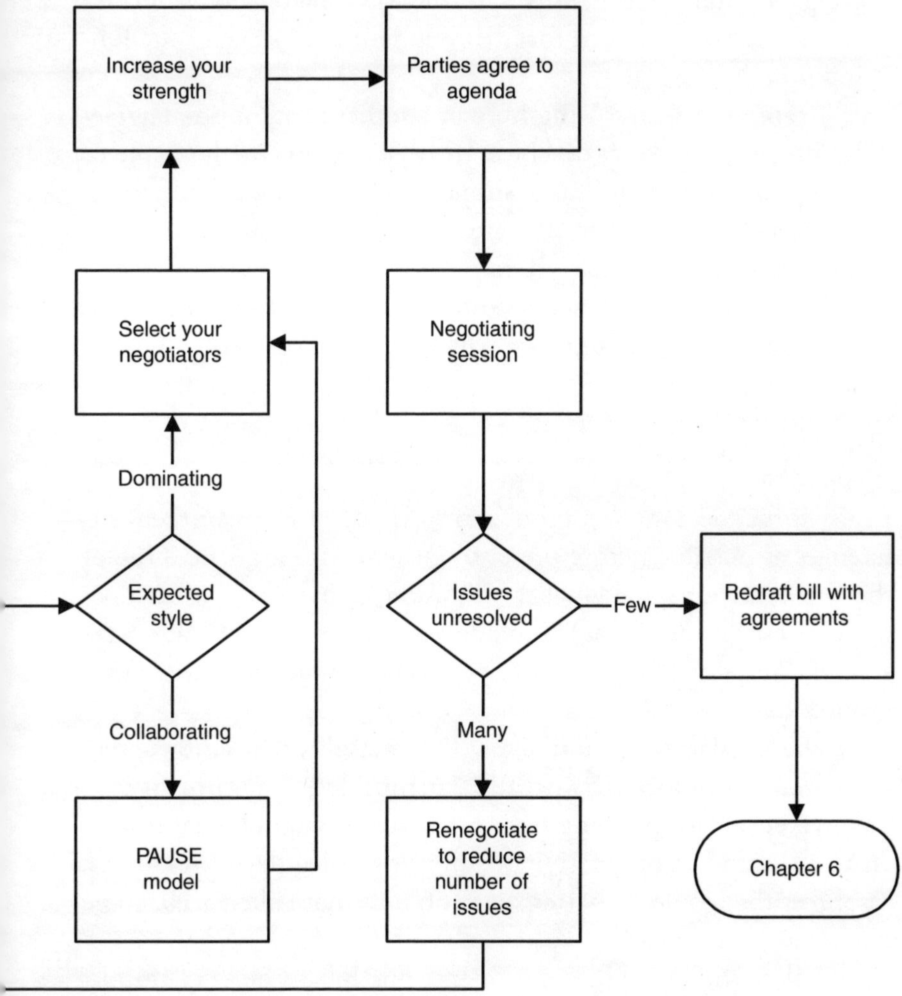
Increase your strength
Parties agree to agenda
Select your negotiators
Negotiating session
Dominating
Expected style
Issues unresolved
Few
Redraft bill with agreements
Collaborating
Many
PAUSE model
Renegotiate to reduce number of issues
Chapter 6

At some time in life, each of us has bargained with someone over the sales price of a house or a car, or when deciding upon a restaurant for dinner. The give-and-take surrounding this process of finding a mutually satisfactory agreement is called negotiation and you will encounter a need for it throughout each stage of the lobbying process.

Negotiation is resolving human conflict using mutual agreement or compromise. It describes the dynamic in which people or groups with different initial positions reach agreement upon a single mutually held position. Usually, the final position is comprised of elements from each party's starting position. The strongest and most long lasting agreements come from negotiations in which both sides enter freely and give willingly in order to reach resolution.

Why negotiate?

Legislators expect interest groups to work out as many of their differences as possible before presenting them with an issue. One of the first questions a lawmaker will ask a lobbyist is, "What does (an interest group's name) think about your bill?" You must have a ready response based upon your communication with that group.

The legislature is more likely to enact bills that enjoy agreement and support than bills surrounded by controversy. Lawmakers avoid spending time on controversial bills that threaten to consume disproportionate amounts of legislative resources; resources that could be better spent on bills more likely to become law.

Unless the legislature considers your bill to be very important, legislators will not spend the limited amount of time in the session negotiating over more than a couple of points. Therefore, before going to the legislature, you must try to find agreement with other groups interested in your bill on as many points as possible. You will not reach complete agreement with all groups on each point, but by building as much agreement as possible, it is more likely that your bill will becomc law.

Who will I negotiate with?

Negotiating begins when your association members seek to define their legislative problem, reach association consensus, gain member commitment to the lobbying effort, organize the lobbying campaign, draft the bill, and possibly hire a contract lobbyist. As your bill continues to progress, you will negotiate internally to respond to amendments proposed by the legislature and others.

After your association has written the bill, but before its introduction into the legislature, you will negotiate with special interest groups who could be affected should your bill become law. Your goal will be to maximize their support or minimize their opposition. Although you must achieve consensus among members within your own association, with interest groups external to the association you will reach only varying degrees of agreement.

State and private sources provide detailed information about state associations that can help you discover the interest groups that might be concerned about your bill.[1] Once you identify them, develop a list that ranks each group based upon *your* estimate of *their* likely level of interest in or concern about your bill. You may never know the accuracy of your evaluation, but this should not prevent you from completing this important activity. As you develop your list of rank-ordered groups, consider:

1. The likelihood that your bill will become law
2. The effect of your bill on the interest group, if it becomes law
3. For each group, the importance of your bill relative to their other bills of interest this session

The actions taken by concerned interest groups may be affected by many factors. For example, if a group with interest in your bill expects a busy legislative session to deal with more pressing matters than your bill, they may not give you much attention. Some groups will not have sufficient political resources to work on your bill in addition to their other bills of interest. On the other hand, if your bill impacts a group greatly, especially if they have few other legislative issues in the session, they may be very interested and give your issue much attention.

As your bill advances though the legislative process, you may find yourself negotiating with persons you never considered. For example, with or without your consent, legislators may combine your bill with one or more similar bills to form one larger "omnibus" or "train" bill. When this happens, you then find yourself negotiating with the supporters and opponents of the omnibus bill.

Will I negotiate with lawmakers?

Generally, you will not negotiate with lawmakers over your bill for two reasons. First, once your bill is introduced into the legislature, you face a diminished amount of control as the session progresses. No longer is it "your bill." Instead, it is the legislature's bill and they, not you, control it. Legislators look first to your sponsor and then to you as they consider your bill, and they may or may not consult with you during negotiations. Second, lawmakers seldom engage in negotiations over most bills because they have too many of them and too little time.

Hopefully, your sponsor will ask you to assist in negotiations over your bill within the legislature. As she or he negotiates with other legislators on your behalf, your role is to support him or her by lobbying other lawmakers to support your sponsor's position. Use the opportunity to lobby for your bill but make no agreements without first talking to your sponsor.

Sometimes a legislator may ask for your views or your *consent* to his or her proposed changes to the bill. Your support for these changes will increase the political acceptability of the lawmaker's desired changes to other legislators.

When to negotiate

The time to start negotiations depends upon the themes of the forthcoming legislative session, the size and scope of your bill, and its impact upon the affected parties. Small bills with limited impact that fit within the session's legislative theme will require much less negotiation time than large bills that affect many or that do not fit the theme. Reduce as much conflict over your bill as possible *before it is introduced.* A committee chair may not consider a controversial bill that he or she believes will consume a disproportionate amount of committee resources, therefore, you have *until first reading* to minimize the disputes over your bill to a few items that a committee can consider quickly.

Building momentum through negotiation

A focused series of negotiations can be used to build momentum for your bill. Once you have identified and ranked the groups likely interested in your bill, approach them to begin to build agreement and support. Start with the interest group most likely to provide active support. Most groups will support you actively if they see personal benefit and have the political resources needed. Once you have gained support from one group, it will be easier for other like-minded groups to also provide support. Work systematically down your list until you reach those groups who will support you passively. Some groups will support your issue passively because, although they agree with your goals, they have more important issues to lobby during the legislative session. As you see the momentum of support begin to build, move lastly to those groups who likely oppose you, starting with the group whose opposition is the weakest. This strategy can result in building considerable political momentum in support of your bill.

Although most negotiation occurs before the legislative session begins and *in the early part* of the session, you will negotiate with interest groups throughout the session to gain and keep support and minimize opposition. As you negotiate with others, you will find two broad categories of negotiating styles.

Negotiation styles[2]

Two frequently used negotiating styles in lobbying are *dominating* and *collaborating.* Each style uses a very different dynamic of human interaction and each proceeds to reach agreement using different techniques. In practice, you may see one style used exclusively or you may see a mixture of both.

The dominating style

The dominating style is encountered most frequently within associations where one member has a disproportionate amount of power over its team members or is disproportionately important to the success of the association and demands its own way. For example, in an association of hospitals, one large regional hospital may threaten to withdraw from the association unless the smaller community hospitals agree to accept their legislative preference. The smaller hospitals may bend to the demands of the bigger institution in order to keep the purchasing advantages conferred by membership in the association.

The dominating style produces fragile alliances because team members are often coerced to make decisions. A dominating negotiator may offer arguments to members of the team, but the reasons given to justify his or her position are really veiled ultimatums. Members and associations surrender to, rather than voluntarily partner with, the dominating style negotiator's positions or requests.

The dominating style of negotiation builds vulnerability, illegitimacy, and weakness into a coalition. If the dominating negotiator's tactics are publicly exposed, the social distaste for bullying can free the weaker parties from the agreements they were forced to make. Those who consider using the dominating style should ask themselves, what would the public reaction be if their negotiating session were to be shown on the evening news? Because dominating negotiators rely on power rather than sound public policy or equity, public and legislative disapproval may greet the arguments they advance to support their position. The threat of public exposure can be used to reduce the effectiveness of this style.

The collaborating style

The most frequently used negotiation style in lobbying is collaborating. Collaborating style negotiations occur most often among parties who are independent of each other. This independence allows them to negotiate freely as peers on the issues.

Agreements forged through collaboration tend to be politically sturdy because the parties reach voluntary agreements that are not influenced by forces unrelated to an issue. Legislators expect parties to adhere to their commitments when they freely enter into agreements with one another. In collaborating style negotiations, no party can withdraw from an agreement unless bad faith is discovered or unless provisions in the bill that had been negotiated change considerably. The PAUSE model offers a good framework for implementing the collaborating style.

The PAUSE model

In *The Peacemaker* (Baker Books, 1997), author Ken Sande proposes a collaborating style for reaching agreement. Called PAUSE, the acronym stands for Prepare, Affirm Relationships, Understand Interests, Search for Creative Solutions, and Evaluate Options

Objectively and Reasonably. Sande's approach embodies the collaborating style in which it is important to balance the principles and interests of all parties. Sande recommends using these to reach agreement.

Prepare

Get the facts, identify issues and interests, use ethical principles, develop options, anticipate reactions, plan an alternative to a negotiated agreement, select an appropriate time and place to meet, plan opening remarks, and seek counsel.

Affirm Relationships

Communicate in a courteous manner, spend time on personal issues before moving to material issues, respect the authority of leaders, earnestly seek to understand by asking sincere questions about what the other negotiators are thinking and feeling, discuss their responses, advance the public interest and interests of others by seeking solutions that really satisfy the needs and desires of all, confront in a gracious manner, allow face-saving, and give praise and thanks for valid points.

Understand Interests

Distinguish interests from positions. An interest is an identifiable and concrete question that must be addressed in order to reach an agreement. A position is a desired outcome or definable perspective on an issue. To find a ready resolution, focus on interests rather than positions.

Ask questions to determine how your interests and those of the other parties coincide or conflict. The more fully you understand the interests of others, the more persuasive and effective you will be when negotiating. Understand your own interests and use caution in revealing them.

Search for Creative Solutions

Spontaneously invent solutions by throwing out ideas that might satisfy needs. Try to "expand the pie" by bringing in additional interests which might be satisfied.

Evaluate Options Objectively and Reasonably

Keep an open and fair mind when negotiating and do not let the negotiation degenerate into a battle of wills. Try to use rules of reason, laws, ethics, or religious principles to evaluate options. Try to discover the hidden reasons behind objections and positions. Look for points that you can give up easily, for matters on which you cannot bend, for issues your opponents can and cannot give up easily, and for points on which you can both agree.

Selecting your negotiator

Negotiating is much more of an art than it is a science. Credentials, expertise, and titles, while valuable, cannot take the place of talents, training, and most of all, negotiating experience. If one of your association members has experience, your selection of a negotiator may be easy. However, if none is available, consider these points in the selection process.

1. A negotiator must be able to withstand the use of rudeness, disapproval, and other psychological techniques.
2. A negotiator must handle rejection well. The most common response to your proposals will be "no." A negotiator who seeks personal approval from others may unconsciously sacrifice your position to avoid rejection by the other negotiators.
3. Good negotiators ask for more than they need.
4. Effective negotiators do not equate failure with not getting all that they want. Persons who fear failure will aim low and accept less in order to avoid feeling defeated.

5. Successful negotiation requires determination. Your representative must be able to return again and again to a matter. He or she must not stop at "no" and must be able to say "no" as often as needed.
6. A good negotiator is likable and remains pleasant even in unpleasant circumstances. It is harder to be rude to a nice person than it is to an unpleasant one.
7. A good negotiator is calm and will not lose sight of his or her goals.
8. Negotiation requires creative thinking. A successful negotiator finds common ground on which to reach agreement.
9. An effective negotiator is a person of integrity, honesty, and fairness. The more trustworthy your negotiator, the more credible he or she will be with other parties.

Increasing your relative strength as a negotiator

Your effectiveness in negotiations will first be affected by the other parties' perception of your political, and therefore your negotiating, strength relative to theirs. The strong often think that they do not need to take seriously, much less negotiate with, the weak. By using some simple tactics, you can increase your relative strength as a negotiator or may force dominating negotiators to become more collaborative.

You can increase your negotiating strength by shifting the style of negotiation from dominating to collaborating. The dominating style relies on power to advance while the collaborating relies on reason, fair play, and advocates on behalf of the public good.

A weaker party can neutralize a dominating style negotiator by holding the negotiating session within the view of the legislature. When forced to negotiate in the public eye, the dominating style will be greatly moderated or entirely replaced by the collaborating.

You can ask an important lawmaker or member of a key committee of referral to express in writing or in person his or her interest in the conduct, outcome, and report of negotiation. This strategy weakens the dominating style.

Ask your main sponsor to inform the other party that he or she will take action on the agreements made in the negotiation session. Then ask him or her to *delegate* his or her authority as a member of the legislature to you for the session. This will cause the other party to face the power your sponsor has "delegated" to you in addition to your own as you negotiate.

Controversy can defeat a bill because lawmakers want to spend time on bills more likely to become law than on those where time will be spent unproductively. It is easier to defeat a bill than to pass it. You can use this fact as you negotiate with a party who wants a bill.

As it appears that your bill is more likely to become law, your negotiating strength will increase. Opponents concerned that your bill may become law will now have greater incentive to negotiate a bill they can live with. They know that they can avoid damage to their interests by acting now. So, although they oppose you, they will negotiate for a bill less damaging to their interests.

As your bill continues to move forward in the legislature, those who were previously uninterested in it may see it as a potential vehicle to carry their own stalled issues to enactment. If they can amend their bill to yours, they will become interested in working with you to see your bill to enactment. Their added support against opponents and as lobbyists brings additional strength to your combined bills.

You may also increase your negotiating strength by using strong or experienced negotiators to represent your issue. A good negotiator who represents a weaker association gains advantage over a poor negotiator who represents a stronger one.

Determining alternative positions

In a negotiation session, your starting position is your ideal bill. Your final position is that point at which you break off negotiations because you cannot compromise further. A series of decreasingly acceptable alternatives to your ideal bill will be found between these two points. These are your alternative positions.

You must determine the place at which you will break off negotiations. What must the legislature enact in order to make your lobbying effort worthwhile? What is failure? What steps will you take if your legislative effort does not succeed? You must clearly identify your break off point. Negotiators who lack a clear point at which to break off negotiations may not know where to stop giving in to the other party's demands and may damage your lobbying effort.

Throughout the legislative process you will be asked to make concessions, accept the "middle ground," choose between competing positions, add and delete bill language, and change bill provisions. With this in mind, try to identify and rank order all of your alternative positions before they are proposed by you or by another party. As you evaluate each alternative, identify the strengths and limitations. Then, when you or the other party proposes an alternative, you can maintain momentum in the negotiation session because you already know the ramifications of each one.

Alternative positions must not be viewed by your negotiator as equivalently acceptable positions. Make him or her aware of the rank ordering of acceptable alternatives and urge the negotiator to aim high. Inexperienced negotiators often seek the path of least resistance, and the outcome least difficult to achieve is often the one accomplished most.

Another strategy that you can use is to give your negotiator no alternatives. Sometimes negotiators work best when given no alternatives to the ideal bill since an "all-or-none" position forces them to make their greatest effort or risk failure.

Preparing for the negotiating session

Regardless of the negotiating style that you encounter, you must be ready for the actual meeting in which you will try to find agreement. Preparation increases the likelihood of achieving your goals. Consider these points when preparing for a negotiating session:

1. Know your association's lobbying goals and overall strategy. Commit them to memory so that you can better focus the negotiation on what is important to the association.
2. Memorize your bill.
3. Memorize your alternative position(s), if any.
4. Determine your political strength and the strength of the other parties because strength greatly affects the willingness to negotiate. If you are the stronger, you may have little reason to make concessions to the politically weaker. If you are the weaker, look for strategies to increase your political strength.
5. Determine the other parties' likely positions and supporting information. What do they want? How will they justify their positions? By identifying their needs and supporting rationale beforehand, you can identify ways to satisfy or counter their concerns.
6. Determine the interests you share with the other parties. Shared interests may include relationships, legislative goals, social, economic, and environmental concerns. Shared interests promote harmony and a favorable disposition toward working together.
7. Identify your low value interests that might be of higher value to the other parties and identify their low value interests that might be of higher value to you.

8. Learn as much as possible about the other negotiator(s). What are their reputations and experiences? Who are their other clients, association members, and allied interest groups?
9. Propose an agenda for the negotiation session to the other parties. Allocate time to discuss each issue. Include your draft bill as an early discussion item.
10. When scheduling the session, do not allow the other parties to begin negotiations over the telephone. Tell them that you do not have the authority to commit but that your lead negotiator at the session will.
11. Agree to record points of agreement on an easel pad or dry board that is in plain view for all to see. On separate easels, record unresolved issues and those deferred for later discussion.
12. Agree to develop a consensus document from the negotiation session and name one member from each party to draft it together.
13. Mutually decide upon the number of participants that will represent each party at the negotiation session. Try to ensure that each party has the same number of participants and limit them to as few as possible. Being outnumbered is a psychological handicap.
14. Determine whether you and the other negotiators have the authority to commit and reach the level of desired resolution.
15. Before you go into the meeting, designate one person from your team to be the lead negotiator. Only he or she may commit you to a position with the other parties
16. Designate one member from your team to take notes.
17. Agree to tape or video record the negotiation session if dominating style negotiators will be present.
18. Agree upon a neutral location for the meeting to minimize interruptions, distractions, and deny a "home field" advantage to any party.

19. Practice your negotiation.

The negotiating session

You must never forget that all negotiation sessions are contests in which each negotiator competes for the best possible outcome for his or her principal or client. A dominating style negotiation creates a tense environment where emotion can cloud judgment and impair performance. In a collaborating style negotiation, inexperienced parties can be lulled into a false sense of trust that can be exploited to their disadvantage by the other negotiators. Use these guidelines to stay focused and emotionally defused when negotiating.

1. Negotiations begin the moment that parties arrive. Because every word spoken formally or informally in the session is significant to the other parties, you must speak cautiously and with great care. Avoid discussing the bill and the details surrounding it until the session has been formally convened.
2. As the parties arrive, establish the common humanity you share with the other negotiators by discussing neutral topics, such as the weather and weekend activities. This may help you separate issues from personalities later in the meeting.
3. Ensure that the numbers of participants from each party in the negotiation session are as agreed. Failure to abide by earlier agreements shows bad faith on the part of the violating party.
4. Identify the lead negotiator for each party and confirm that he or she has the authority to commit at the level of agreement desired. Cancel the session if there is inadequate authority or state that all resultant agreements will be considered as tentative.
5. Keep your goals and acceptable alternatives to the ideal bill in mind.

6. Keep the point at which you will break off negotiations in mind.
7. As a first item of business review the agenda that you and the other parties developed in advance to guide the negotiating session. This will help you focus and adhere to the time allocated to each topic.
8. Use your draft bill as a template for discussion with the other parties and ask them to identify points of agreement. This may enable you to initially lead the meeting and affect the outcome of the session.
9. Budget your use of "yes" and "no." Because reciprocity characterizes collaborating style negotiation, the other parties expect a "yes" from you in exchange for each "yes" that they give. Sometimes, they may expect you to give a "yes" on the basis of reciprocity rather than on the substance of their request. You must avoid feeling pressured to respond with a "yes" if the substance of their request is unacceptable.
10. Likewise, do not spend one of your "no's" on an outrageous suggestion. Ignore it, smile about it, or record it on the easel as an item for discussion at a later time.
11. Avoid making concessions to the other parties just because they have made concessions to you. Give information or make concessions only when you receive benefit. You can never take back what has been given away.
12. Stay focused on the issues and do not allow others to sidetrack discussions by "being difficult."
13. Remain politely skeptical of the facts, figures, and conclusions presented by other parties. The interpretation of data may sometimes be skewed to yield conclusions not supported by an objective analysis. Freely question the data and their supporting arguments.
14. Never hesitate to ask questions if you cannot understand exactly what somebody is talking about.

15. Remember that you are tied to your spoken word. Give yourself time to process what is happening. Take breaks as needed.
16. Respond slowly to others and do not speak until you are ready. This prevents you from rushing into a bad decision.
17. In plain view of all parties, record the points of agreement, areas of disagreement, and items deferred for later discussion on dry boards or flip charts.
18. Make a common set of notes using the dry boards or flip charts from the meeting. Charge a team that consists of one representative from each party with the responsibility to draft a consensus document. If possible, distribute this draft for comments from all participants during the meeting. If not possible, distribute it as soon as you are able.
19. Depart promptly and amicably and do not linger with the other parties. Until you are alone and well outside of the building, avoid conversation even among yourselves about the negotiation session. Do not allow small talk with the other parties to be used to reopen negotiations. Remember that every time you discuss your issue, you are re-negotiating it.
20 In private, review the events of the meeting with each person in your party and plan the next steps to take.

Negotiating tricks and techniques to counter them —

Some negotiators will use "tricks" to gain an advantage although few, if any, are used in good faith, collaborating style negotiations. Here are some tricks and suggested techniques to help you counter them based, in part, upon the work of negotiating pioneer Chester Karrass.

1. Intimidating environment. The other party may offer or even insist that you hold negotiations in his or her offices. Negotiating on the "home court" creates an intimidating and often uncomfortable environment. You should insist that a

neutral environment, such as a hotel conference room, be used for negotiations.

2. Exceeding the number of negotiators agreed upon. Insist on adherence to prior commitments that limit all parties to the agreed upon number of attendees or do not negotiate.
3. Rudeness. Rudeness is used to unnerve you into making concessions to escape hostility. Rudeness is an especially useful tool against collaborating style negotiators. Confront rudeness directly and ask if it is the negotiator's technique. If he or she continues, ignore it, complain to a higher authority about it, or tell the other party that you will leave until such time as a civil negotiator is substituted for the rude one.
4. Good cop/bad cop. This is a version of the rudeness technique. While one of the other party's negotiators (the bad cop) badgers you, his or her teammate (the good cop) appears to constrain the bad cop and offers to mediate a reasonable agreement. If you will not yield on important points, the good cop says that he or she will have no choice but to leave you to negotiate again with the uncivil teammate. Do not let the good cop/bad cop game start. At the first clear sign of rudeness, respond as in number three above.
5. Disapproval. Verbally and non-verbally, the other party may send a message of disapproval to shame, embarrass, or humiliate you for not agreeing to his or her "reasonable" demands. Counter disapproval by sending a negotiator to the session who does not equate personal approval from the other parties with success.
6. Wasting time. To force last minute desperate concessions as time is running out, one party may refuse to follow the agenda and may consistently exceed time allocations. To counter this trick, insist on adherence to the original agenda and its allotted times at first sign of time wasting.

7. Introducing new demands. A party may try to insert new demands or place a new item on the agenda. This can be avoided by establishing and adhering to the agenda. As the negotiation session begins, review the agenda to limit the issues that will be considered at the meeting.
8. Making extreme demands. A party may ask for more than is reasonable or make outrageous statements. Respond by appealing to fairness and remind him or her that the legislature will not adopt bills that contain unfair agreements.
9. No alternatives to the first offer. This trick tries to force you into accepting a no-discussion, "take it or leave it" position. Counter by asking the other party to explain how it arrived at its position. Then look for weaknesses in reasoning as the rationale is explained.
10. Threatening and bluffing. This trick threatens to bring consequences unrelated to your bill. For example, a party may threaten to move its facility to another state if your bill is enacted. Counter the threats by protesting and ask the party to reveal the facts that support the statements.
11. Sellout panic. The other party may claim that your allies are about to "sell you out" and urge you to protect your interests by reaching an agreement now. Avoid this trick by communicating regularly with your allies to confirm that no conflicts exist.
12. Suddenly no authority. As a negotiating session concludes, a party's lead negotiator may unexpectedly announce that another principal must approve the agreement in order for it to become effective. This causes the negotiated agreement to degrade into an offer that can later be accepted or rejected in part or in full by the other parties. Avoid this maneuver by asking all parties to reveal their level of authority to bind their organizations before negotiations begin.

13. Ask for more and expect to settle for less. Each side assumes the other is doing this, and each probably is.

Karrass suggests that when you see a trick being used, ask the user what he or she thinks the gain will be. By demonstrating awareness, you may discourage further trickery.

Remember that you can always walk out of a negotiation session. The other parties are not going to physically restrain you. If the other parties are trying to subvert the negotiation, let them know you that will walk away if necessary and that you will bring to the sponsor and legislature the facts that prompted your departure. The other parties may lose if negotiations cease. Ask the offending party if exposing their maneuvers will cause the legislature to label them as acting in bad faith. If you have taped the negotiating session, you will have the evidence. The threat of public exposure for unfairness and consequent legislative disapproval may sober them.

Let's meet halfway

Because issues often remain unresolved as the negotiation session concludes, the other parties may offer to meet you "halfway" to resolve them. Agreeing to a seemingly "fair" offer can get for you or the other parties fifty to one hundred percent of what could not be obtained earlier.

For quantitative items such as money and time, a fifty-fifty split can be easily calculated. For qualitative issues, however, calculating the split is usually more difficult and may lead to, "I'll give you your way on this matter if you give me my way on that other matter." Remember that the reason an issue was not resolved earlier in the negotiation was because an acceptable agreement could not be reached within the allotted time. Splitting up the unresolved issues at the end of the session can be productive but dangerous. Be aware that other parties may agree to give you a small issue and "in the spirit of fairness," demand your concession on a big one. Problems arise when negotiators focus on splitting the items on a list rather than thinking about their relative importance.

What if you and your opponents cannot agree?

Negotiators may not be able to agree on one or more provisions in a draft bill. When this happens, the two sides should clearly identify the points on which they do agree and those on which they do not. Legislators expect that a few issues will remain unresolved following negotiation sessions. As long as all parties have acted in good faith to resolve as many issues as possible, the negotiation process has worked.

After negotiating, you should bring to the legislature a revised version of the bill that incorporates all of the provisions that were agreed to as well as a list of those points on which consensus could not be reached. The value of consensus among special interest groups affected by your bill cannot be overemphasized. However, keep in mind that the ratification of your agreement by the legislature, while highly likely, is not certain.

Summary

You will start negotiating as soon as you try to gain consensus among your association members in the earliest stages of the proposed lobbying project. Negotiating skills will also be used when working with interest groups that support and oppose you. Throughout the lobbying campaign, you will negotiate repeatedly within your association and with interest groups. And if executive agency rule making follows, you will find yourself negotiating with agency officials and interest groups.

Now that the fundamentals of preparing to meet the legislature have been addressed, you must give time and attention to learning legislative procedure. Your involvement with each procedural step will help your bill meet prescribed deadlines and may prevent it from being overlooked by the legislature.

---

1 For example, Columbia Books, Inc., 1212 New York Ave., N.W. Suite 330 Washington, D.C. (202) 898-0662, www.d-net.com/columbia publishes the names and information about United States' trade associations at both the state and federal levels.

2 A number of excellent books about how to negotiate have been written. Scholars have identified several models of negotiating styles. For a valuable study of negotiating and several styles see, Roger Fisher and William Ury, *Getting to Yes,* Penguin Books (1983). Chester Karrass, the dean of business negotiation, has written a number of excellent books including *The Negotiating Game,* Harper Business (1992). Paul Lisnek's *Winning the Mind Game,* Meta Publications (1996) emphasizes relationship building in reaching agreements. The author acknowledges his debt to these scholars.

PART II

Making Ideas Into Law

6 Legislative Procedure

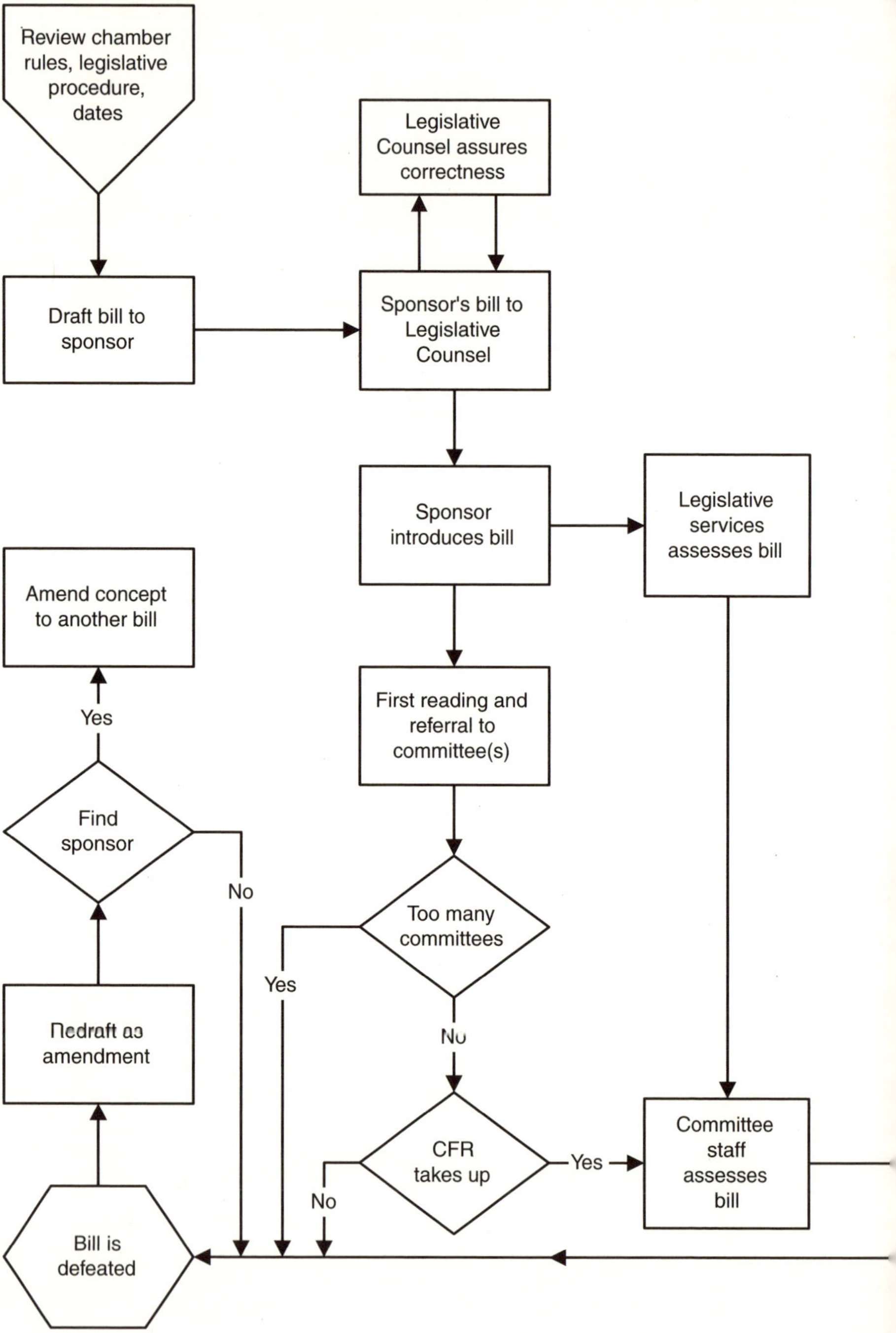

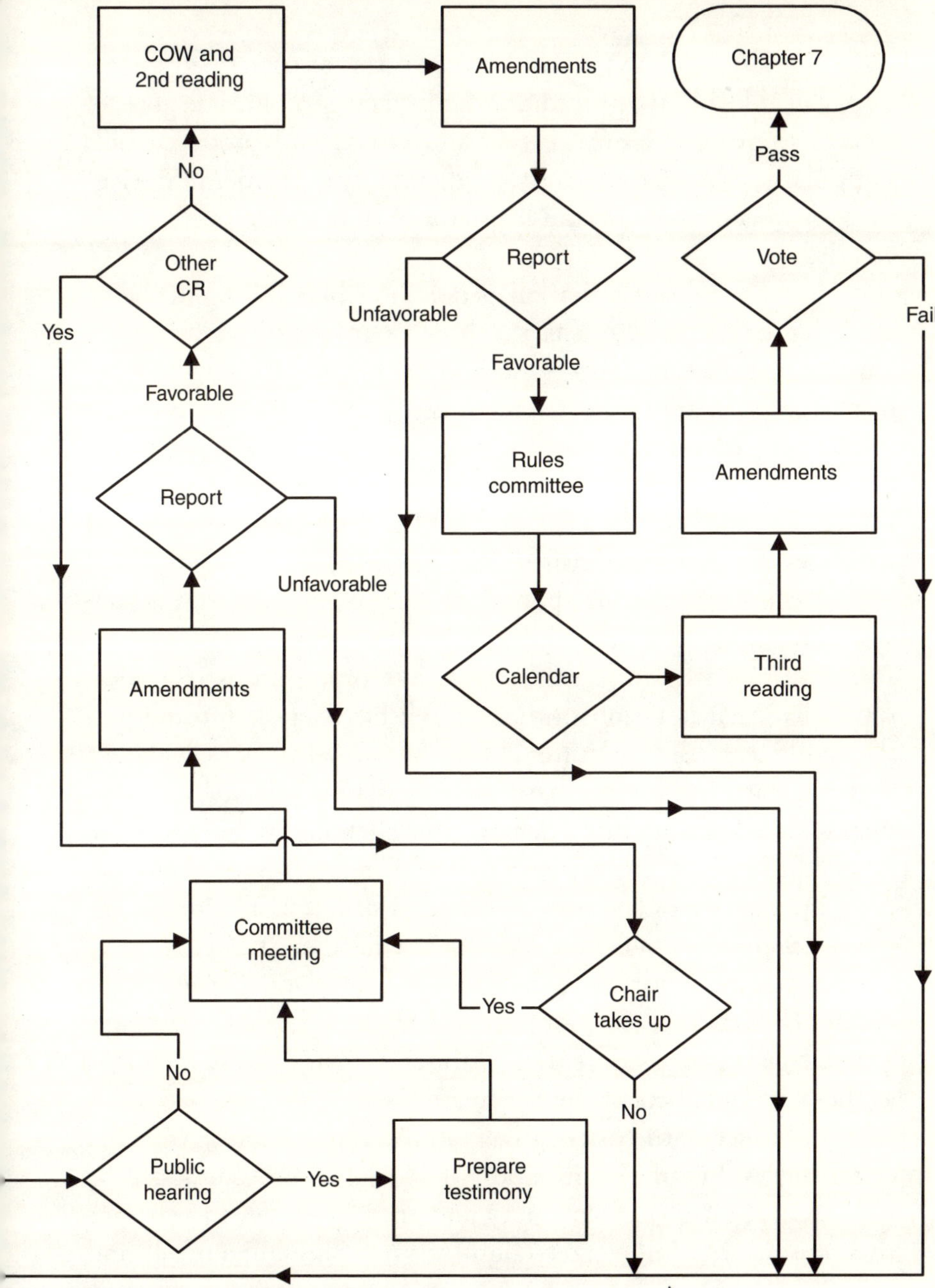

Note: CR = committee of referral CFR = committee of first referral,

COW = committee of the whole

The legislature follows a standardized series of prescribed formal steps called legislative procedure when enacting a bill. The goals of legislative procedure are to treat all persons and proposed bills impartially, provide uniformity, predictability and order in the legislative process, and use the legislature's time and resources efficiently.

Procedure ensures that all people and bills follow the same sequence of steps, it opens the process to public view, and it ensures that each interest group and lawmaker receives the same opportunity to argue the merits of his or her bill. The intended result of procedure is fairness and integrity in the legislative process.

The path your bill will travel is filled with people, rules, and timelines that must be satisfied. Your knowledge of procedure will enable you to help your sponsor to keep your bill from a fatal stumbling along the way.

The first step in learning legislative procedure is to understand that each state constitution establishes a legislature and presiding officers. All legislatures consist of two groups of lawmakers and all state legislatures have two legislative *chambers*, except Nebraska, which has only a Senate. One chamber in the legislature is called the Senate or "Upper House." Senators serve a four-year term in most states and a two-year term in a few. The other legislative chamber is called the House, Assembly, or "Lower House." House members, variously called Representatives, Delegates, or Assembly Members serve a two-year legislative term. On average, a state legislature has two to three times as many House members as there are members of the Senate.

You must learn basic legislative procedure to lobby your bill effectively. While the entire body of legislative procedure can be very complex with parliamentary and chamber rules, the sections that you need to know are straightforward. Should your bill find itself in the unusual circumstance of being the subject of a complex parliamentary process, your sponsor will assist you. However, you need to know basic procedures in order to monitor the progress of your bill and to help your sponsor to keep your bill from a defeat or delay along the way.

Legislative officers

Presiding Officers

Each state's constitution establishes two presiding officers, one for each chamber. Lobbyists are interested in the presiding officers because among many other activities, they:

1. Appoint the chairs, vice-chairs, and members of committees
2. Establish the calendar for legislative activities
3. Refer bills to committees
4. Chair the chamber sessions
5. Authenticate all official acts of the chamber by his or her signature

The leader of the Senate is called the *President.* In most states, the Senate elects its President while in others, the Lieutenant Governor is constitutionally appointed as President. The President appoints or the chamber elects a *President pro Tempore* to serve in his or her absence. The presiding officer in the House is called the *Speaker* and he or she is elected by the chamber. The *Speaker pro Tempore* is appointed by the Speaker or elected by the chamber to serve in his or her absence.

The legislature and political parties elect or appoint a number of offices not established by the state constitution. The legislature identifies and may change the positions, duties, and terms of office for the non-constitutional officers as needed.

Majority Leader or Majority Floor Leader

The majority political party selects the Majority Leader to represent it on the floor of the chamber. He or she may make parliamentary motions, points of order, or take actions from the floor that the President or Speaker, as the presiding officer, may not take. When the Lieutenant Governor is the President, the Majority Leader is the effective leader of the Senate.

Minority Leader or Minority Floor Leader

The Minority Leader is selected by the minority political party to serve as its leader on the floor. He or she works with the presiding officer, majority party leader, and majority party to ensure that the concerns of the minority party and their constituents are heard. When the Lieutenant Governor is President and is a member of the minority party, the Minority Leader may take actions on the floor for the President.

Committee Chairs

The chairs of committees have tremendous power to influence the survival of a bill. Each may decide whether the committee will hear a bill, whether or not supporters and opponents will be allowed to testify, and may assign a bill to a subcommittee for further consideration.

Clerk of the House and Secretary of the Senate

The executive assistant in the House is usually called the *Clerk* and the executive assistant in the Senate is usually called the *Secretary.* These non-legislative officers are elected by each chamber or appointed by the President or Speaker to complete clerical duties. These officers hire staff to help them read and log-in bills, maintain the chamber journal, proofread amendments, track bill progress, engross and enroll bills, and maintain smooth operation of the chamber.

Sergeant-at-Arms

The Sergeant-at-Arms helps the President or Speaker maintain order in the chamber, bars unauthorized persons from the floor, announces and carries messages, and delivers orders issued by the chamber commanding attendance at official meetings. He or she also hires assistants, such as Doorkeepers.

Ethics Office

This office is charged with enforcing lobbyist registration and reporting requirements. Failure to comply with state ethics requirements can lead to punishment in the form of fines or loss of lobbying privileges.

Legislative services agencies

These agencies are non-partisan offices that draft bills or ensure that bills drafted by others meet requirements for legality, form, and style so they may be introduced. They also ensure that bills do not conflict with existing state or federal law. They produce staff analyses of fiscal, legal, social, environmental, and other impacts of proposed legislation.

Committee and personal staff

Each committee likely has clerical staff and technical staff. Legislators may have personal staff.

Chamber rules

Each state constitution stipulates the basic rules of the legislature; the terms and qualifications of legislators, dates and time allowed for legislative sessions, the effective dates for laws, and other foundational provisions. State constitutions impose requirements on the legislature that range from very basic to detailed instructions.

The legislature adopts its rules by resolution at the beginning of each biennium,[1] and changes to the rules may occur at two-year intervals. Each chamber adopts its own rules, and the Senate and House often adopt "Joint Rules" to govern interactions between the two chambers. Chamber rules govern the organization of the chamber, establish committees and officers, define the operation of the chamber, and govern the conduct of members, employees, and visitors.

Legislative procedures are embedded within the chamber rules. Do not expect to find a section within the rules entitled "legislative procedure." Legislative procedures are scattered among the rules, and if you gathered them into a single unit, they would fill approximately six pages or less.

Although most chamber rules will not affect your lobbying effort, you should read all of them to gain a sense of how the chamber functions. Then, isolate and study those rules related to bill enactment. If the legislature fails to follow the correct procedures, your bill may be prevented from further consideration. Although the legislature alone is charged with the responsibility to follow the prescribed legislative procedures, your knowledge of procedure will enable you to identify problems related to your bill's progress.

Remember that your bill can get lost among the thousands of other bills that the legislature faces in a session. Stay involved with your bill's progress as a "quality control" agent for your sponsor. Work closely with him or her and with the other legislators to ensure that your bill meets all deadlines and follows the required procedural steps.

Other legislative procedures

In addition to legislative procedures, other formal rules and informal traditions govern the operation of the chamber. When the state constitution, statutes, rules of the legislature, or chamber rules provide insufficient guidance for dealing with a particular situation, then standard manuals of legislative or parliamentary procedure may be consulted. These references include *Mason's Manual of Legislative Procedure, Jefferson's Manual of Parliamentary Procedure,* and *Robert's Rules of Order.* The references used may differ between each Senate and House as well as among all fifty state legislatures.

Special rules are adopted to deal with specific matters, such as the amount of time allowed to debate a particular piece of legislation. Special rules improve the efficiency of the legislature because they enable it to individualize procedure for unusual situations. Special rules may or may not affect your bill.

Critical dates

Each state constitution and legislature establish critical dates consonant with the steps for a bill becoming law. Because the time and scope of legislative sessions are limited, your bill must meet each deadline. The failure to meet even one of them may cost you your bill. Although the presiding officer and chamber can suspend or revise timelines by super majority vote, suspensions are usually made on a case-by-case basis. You cannot rely on a suspension of timelines to save your bill if it falls behind in meeting critical dates.

How your bill becomes law - a generic model

Once you have written your bill and enlisted your main sponsor, you are ready to introduce it in accord with a prescribed series of steps for all bills. Described is a composite derived from the practices of many different states. Let it serve as a generic model to help you learn how bills become laws. A more complete description of each step in the model will follow.

1. The legislature's bill drafting service composes the bill.
2. Legislative Counsel assures that the bill's legality and form are correct.
3. The main sponsor introduces the bill in his or her chamber, called the chamber or house of origin.
4. Legislative services agency staff evaluates and reports on the bill's proposed impacts: social, environmental, economic, and other.
5. First reading of the bill.
6. Bill is sent to committee(s) of referral.
7. Committee staff evaluates and reports on the bill to the committee.
8. Committee(s) consider(s) the bill, proposes amendments, if any.
9. Committee(s) report(s) the bill to the entire chamber.
10. Committee of the Whole considers the bill, proposes amendments, if any.
11. Second reading of the bill, debate, and amendment.
12. Approval by Legislative Counsel or Rules Committee and scheduling of the amended bill for third reading.
13. Third reading of the bill and chamber vote.
14. If approved, chamber of origin engrosses the bill and sends it to the other chamber.
15. Action is taken by the receiving chamber on the bill.
16. Both chambers resolve differences, if any, over the bill and enroll it.
17. Legislature sends the enactment to the Governor.
18. Governor, vetoes, approves,[2] or does nothing with the bill.
19. If vetoed, the legislature sustains the veto, overrides the Governor's veto, amends the enactment to suit the Governor, lets it die, or sues in court to nullify the veto.
20. The enactment becomes an act.
21. The act becomes law upon publication in public records.

Now that you have reviewed the generic model, it is important to realize that all states do not use all steps nor do all states follow the same order of steps. Most publish a flowchart that describes the steps for a bill to become a law in that state. This chart may be obtained from the Internet or chamber Clerk's offices.

1. Bill drafting

Bills must be legally correct and presented in a form established by the legislature. The legislature's Legislative Counsel, Bill Drafting Services, or legislative services agency provides this service. All bills must meet the legislature's standards for use of terms, recitations, bill summaries, citing of statutes, and other requirements. In some states, the sponsor's request to draft the bill is assigned a number that identifies the bill throughout its legislative life.

2. Legislative Counsel

The Legislative Counsel, Revisor of Statutes, Rules Committee, or similar office approves bills and their amendments for form and legal sufficiency. A legislative services agency composes the bill summary that appears on the bill. A certification of inspection that the bill does not conflict with constitutional or statutory requirements may be required for introduction.[3]

3. Main sponsor introduces bill

The bill is introduced into one or both chambers. The main sponsor in a chamber submits the bill to the Bill Clerk who is charged with receiving new bills. The Bill Clerk assures that the submitted bill is in accord with the chamber's rules, enters the bill into the logbook, and assigns it a bill number. In general, only members of the chamber may sponsor or co-sponsor a bill. Other sponsors and co-sponsors register their support of the bill by signing written documentation of sponsorship.

Companion bills are identical twins; one bill is introduced in the House and the other is introduced in the Senate. Companion bills may be introduced simultaneously in each chamber or at different times during the legislative session. Concurrent consideration of twin bills by both chambers shortens the time needed to evaluate a bill during the limited legislative session. Companion bills may enable a bill to pass between both chambers before expiration of the legislative session.

Each companion bill must have its own sponsor in each chamber. Because enactment requires approval of an identical bill by both chambers, lobbyists and sponsors in each chamber must coordinate activities to keep the companion bills identical.

A chamber may limit the number of co-sponsors on a bill or may limit each legislator to a specified maximum number of bills that he or she may introduce in a session. Make sure each prospective sponsor or co-sponsor has a bill allocation remaining for you.

4. Legislative services agency evaluates and reports on the bill

This office evaluates the bill and predicts its likely impacts on the state should it become law. Areas studied for impact include economic, environmental, social, governmental, and state budgetary. The report of this office may affect the chances of bill enactment.

5. First reading

A bill must be *read* and approved at least three times over three different days by the majority of each chamber before it can become a law.[4] The first reading often consists of printing the bill number and title in the chamber journal or reading this same information to the chamber. In addition, there may be a short description or summary of the bill.[5]

6. Bill referred to committees

After first reading, the chamber leader refers the bill to committees. Bills are *referred* (assigned) to at least one or possibly more committees[6] called *committees of referral.* Each committee may consider only the bills referred to it. The committee that each bill starts with is called the *committee of first referral* and is the committee with jurisdiction over the bill's subject matter. Environmental bills begin with the Environment Committee, agricultural bills with the Agricultural Committee, and so forth. You will work most closely with the committee of first referral. A bill not referred to a committee is defeated.

Depending on the content of your bill, it may be referred to additional committees that review it following the committee of first referral.[7] Your goal should be to avoid referrals to unfavorable committees and minimize the number of referrals to subsequent committees so that you can reduce the opportunities for unfavorable amendments, delay, or defeat. This goal is accomplished by skillful bill drafting and communication with the chamber leader. Time works against a bill given multiple referrals because it will not be able to complete the legislative process before the session expires.[8] A bill assigned to unfavorable committees or to too many committees will not be enacted.

7. Committee staff evaluates and reports on bill to committee

Because few legislators are experts in all matters that come before their committees, some states employ professional staff to advise them about technical matters. Committee staff have great influence on the outcome of committee actions on your bill.

8. Committee(s) considers bill, amendments proposed, if any

Although referral to a committee means that your bill is alive, it does not ensure that any more action will be taken on it. Committees of referral, including the committee of first referral, either take up your bill or defeat it through inaction. Many bills are defeated by committee inaction caused by a lack of chair or committee support, disinterest in the bill, dislike of the bill's sponsor, work overload, or other reasons. The failure of your bill to pass through any committee having jurisdiction over it generally means it is defeated.

Your goal is to convince each committee to take favorable action on your bill. You want them to consider your bill, discuss it, amend it as little as possible, and favorably report (pass) it. The committee may hold a hearing on your bill, take testimony, consider amendments, and vote. A unanimous favorable vote results in the chamber leader sending the bill to the consent calendar. A favorable report requires a vote of half of the committee quorum plus one. Each committee passage of your bill builds momentum and increases the probability that it will pass successive committees and the chamber.

9. Committee report to the chamber

Following the favorable votes of all committees of referral, the committee of first referral presents a formal report on your bill to the chamber. This comprehensive report includes a record of hearings, testimony, committee votes, and other committee actions on the bill. The report concludes with a recommendation for chamber action. An unfavorable report usually defeats the bill while a favorable report provides momentum for continuation through the legislative process.[9]

10. Committee of the Whole

Many chambers use this committee which is comprised of all legislators in the chamber.[10] The Committee of the Whole considers your bill, the proposed amendments, the report of the committee of first referral, and information from other committees of referral. The Committee of the Whole may debate the bill and propose additional amendments. The Committee votes upon the bill and proposed amendments and defeats or reports the bill with recommendations to the chamber for consideration during second reading.

11. Second reading by the chamber, including debate and amendment

In second reading, the chamber considers the Committee of the Whole's report, including the proposed amendments, and may debate the bill. After the debate a vote is taken. If the vote is favorable, the bill is sent to third reading. If the bill is extensively amended, it is referred to a committee of referral with subject matter jurisdiction. If the vote at second reading is unfavorable, the bill is defeated.

12. Approval by Legislative Counsel or Rules Committee

Before third reading, the legality of the amended bill is reviewed by the designated office. Staff may prepare another bill analysis to inform the chamber of the meaning and consequences of the final bill, if enacted. The Rules Committee must schedule (calendar) the bill for third reading. If not calendared, the bill is defeated.

13. Third reading and final vote

At third reading, the entire chamber considers your bill for the final time. Since the bill was debated in second reading, some states limit or disallow debate or amendment during third reading. At third reading, the bill is read and a vote is taken. If passed, the bill is certified as having passed the chamber (engrossed). If the vote at third reading is unfavorable, the bill is defeated.[11]

14. Chamber of origin sends the engrossed bill to other chamber

In order to become law, both chambers must approve the identical bill. The chamber from which the bill originated sends (messages) the engrossed bill to the other chamber for consideration and vote.

15. The receiving chamber takes action on the bill

The receiving chamber considers the messaged bill by repeating the entire process (steps 5-13 above) or by sending it to third reading and final chamber vote. If the receiving chamber has considered an identical companion bill, then the process can be shortened considerably.[12] If the receiving chamber approves the engrossed bill without amendments, it returns the bill to the chamber of origin. The signature of the President and Speaker certify it as an enactment (enrolled). If amended by the receiving chamber, the bill is messaged back to the originating chamber for concurrence.

16. Chambers resolve differences on the bill

Although each chamber may approve a different version of the bill, agreement on the same version of the bill by both chambers is required for enactment. Once approved and enrolled, the bill becomes an enactment. If different versions of the bill are approved or if one chamber will not accept the other chamber's version, the bill is defeated.

17. Legislature sends the enactment to the Governor

The legislature messages the enactment to the Governor for his or her action.

18. Action by the Governor

If the Governor signs the enactment, it becomes an *act*. If vetoed, the enactment goes back to the legislature. The Governor may take no action. Depending upon the state, inaction either allows an enactment to become law without the Governor's signature or is the same as a veto.

19. Response of the legislature to the Governor's veto

A super majority of legislators, normally two-thirds of each chamber, may override the Governor's veto. Failure to gain the necessary two-thirds sustains the veto and the bill is defeated. A chamber may sue to have the court declare the veto unconstitutional. In practice, vetoes are seldom overridden and will defeat most bills.

20. Enactment becomes an act without Governor's signature

If inaction constitutes approval or if the legislature overrides the Governor's veto, the enactment becomes an act without his or her signature.

21. Publication of the new law

The act becomes law when published by the Secretary of State in the state's official records and upon reaching the effective date. The effective date is either the date established by the state constitution or is established by the legislature by super majority vote.

Calendaring

The chamber is required to give public notice of its actions. These notices are called *files, lists, orders,* or *calendars.* Each time a bill is to be considered, read, debated, or voted upon, it must be "calendared." Except by super majority vote, a bill not calendared may not be considered by the chamber and is defeated.

Each chamber uses a number of different calendars. The *daily calendar, four-day calendar,* and *advance journal and calendar* announce the expected order of business for a specific forthcoming legislative day. Calendars are distributed twenty-four to ninety-six hours before consideration of listed bills. Because much can change after publishing a calendar, a *supplemental daily calendar* identifies the current day's agenda. The supplemental daily calendar is prepared each morning and may be changed for the day by super majority vote of the chamber.

Of concern to lobbyists, the daily calendar provides notice of bills that passed during the previous day from second to third reading and a variety of bills to be considered on the current day, including:

1. Bills for second reading
2. Bills carried over from the previous day
3. Postponed bills
4. Motions to recall tabled bills
5. Bills vetoed by the Governor that the chamber will try to override
6. Bills from the other chamber
7. Conference committee bills

A daily calendar may also list other chamber activities that will occur. These include committee meetings, public hearings, resolutions, consideration of gubernatorial nominations (Senate), and other items of chamber business.

A *special orders calendar* allows the Rules Committee, Calendar Committee, or by super majority vote, the chamber, to place an item on the calendar for consideration at a specific time and date. This consideration takes precedence over all other scheduled items. Some states use the *general orders* or *special orders calendar* to list the bills for second reading and *special orders* or *bill calendar* to list the bills for third reading.

The consent calendar or consent orders allows non-controversial and local bills to be enacted with the minimum expenditure of legislative energy.[13] It requires unanimous consent of the committees of referral and chamber. If an amendment is demanded or objection is made, the bill is removed from the calendar and sent to second reading. Bills passed on the consent calendar are engrossed and sent to the other chamber.

You will know when activities related to your bill are scheduled because the legislature publishes the chamber's calendar. By reading the calendar, you can know when and where to invest political resources and lobby lawmakers and staff. However, in the waning hours of the session, there is no time for notices. You must be present in the chamber to advocate for your bill if it still has a chance of enactment but has not passed.

The Journal

Each chamber summarizes its floor activities in its *daily journal.* The daily journal enables lobbyists to know about chamber decisions regarding their bill and the procedural plans of the legislature that affect it. At the end of the annual session, the daily journals are bound into the *annual journal* or simply *journal.*

Sessions

The term *session* refers to blocks of time during which the legislature may conduct official business. The term may also refer to the hours during which the legislature meets on a particular day. For example, the legislature will be in session from Tuesday 10 AM until 3 PM. It also refers to the length of time between the first day of the legislative session and the last day or adjournment.

The state constitution may establish three kinds of sessions: organizational, regular, and special. *Organizational sessions* occur shortly after a general election when the legislature organizes itself by electing leaders and taking other administrative actions. *Regular sessions* are established for conducting the normal business of the legislature.[14] Your bill and others will be considered during the regular session. By proclamation, a *special session* may be convened by the Governor or legislature itself.[15] During special sessions, topics for discussion are usually limited to those named in the proclamation.

Pre-sessions

The pre-session is important to lobbyists because, although the entire chamber will not meet, committees may meet and bills may be pre-filed. Although prohibited from meeting as a body in formal session and from enacting legislation, the legislature uses the pre-session to prepare for the forthcoming regular session. You may obtain notices of pre-sessions from the legislature. If your state has pre-session activities, you need to be active on behalf of your bill.

Amending your bill

Remember that once "your" bill is introduced into the legislature, it becomes "their" bill. You lose your ability to control it and others gain the power to amend it. Therefore, you must work closely with your main sponsor and be aware of all committee and floor actions regarding it.

By the time your bill is signed into law, it may look considerably different from the first draft you brought to your sponsor.

Remember that your goal in the legislative process is to enable your concept to become law. You should be less concerned by the fact that your bill has been amended and focus instead on how the subsequent amendments improve or diminish the likelihood of your concept becoming law.

Who will change your bill?

Before introduction into the chamber, your main sponsor may require changes to your bill as a condition of sponsorship. The bill may also be changed by the legislative services agency if found legally deficient. As your bill proceeds through the steps of the legislative process, different individuals will propose amendments. Just as the original bill required a sponsor, so each amendment to your bill must also have its own sponsor.

Those interested in changing your bill will come from two groups. The first will be opponents with whom you negotiated earlier. The issues that you failed to reach agreement on will now be advanced by your opponents' legislative allies. The second interested group is persons who are new to you and your issue. They are opportunists who may have become quite interested in your bill only because it is moving toward enactment. They will see it as a vehicle to carry their stalled bill to the Governor's desk and will try to amend their bill to yours. Do not think harshly of these opportunists because you may need to become one yourself.

The chamber may combine your bill with similar bills to form one big omnibus bill or train. The chamber leadership may assemble a train because it conserves legislative time and energy and the mixing of less attractive with more attractive-to-pass bills makes it more likely that the less attractive bills will become laws.

Remember, too, that if the other chamber amends your bill when it is received from the chamber of origin, the chamber of origin must approve the amended bill in order to enroll it. If your bill was amended unfavorably in committee, you may ask your main sponsor to amend it back to the original version, and if it has stalled, you may ask him or her to amend your concept to a bill that is moving forward.

Technical considerations of amendments

The process of amending a bill varies somewhat among state legislatures. Common to all states is the requirement that an amendment be *germane;* that is, relevant to the topic of the bill being amended.

Amendments may be proposed in written or oral form. When written, the amendment's sponsor must supply the committee secretary or chamber Clerk with a copy to be printed and distributed to the committee or chamber membership. Requirements for oral amendment vary among the states. In some, the Clerk must write out the amendment before the chamber will consider it, while in others the amendment may be considered and voted upon when spoken.

In some states, the legislative services agency or chamber Clerk drafts the amendment. If an amendment substantially changes a bill, then the staff, the committee of origin, or both may complete a revised bill analysis. Substantially amended bills must often return to the committee(s) of referral for consideration.

Amendments are proposed on a word-by-word basis and the amendment sponsor is responsible for proposing the amendment and leading the debate, if any. Each amendment must be adopted individually. Depending upon the state, any member may propose amendments to a bill during the second or sometimes third reading. After all amendments to the bill have been accepted by the committee or chamber, the bill, as amended, is voted upon.

The phrase "amended in committee" is a technical misnomer but practical reality in most states. Only the chamber, not committees, can amend bills. Committees recommend amendments to the chamber.[16] Since ninety-five percent of committee recommendations are accepted, although technically incorrect, in practice a committee *amends* a bill.

Make sure you are lobbying the right bill

Few actions discredit a lobbyist more than working in error from an out-of-date version of the bill. After each session in which the bill is considered and in advance of the next consideration, the chamber prints an engrossed version of the bill. The Bill Historian should contact the Bill Clerk, bill room, chamber printer, or other reliable source to assure that you have the current version of your bill. He or she should retain copies of each version of the bill, copies of amendments, and reasons for bill changes.

Variations of sequence and terminology among states

Remember that state legislatures differ in the terms used to describe the same legislative activity. Also, the sequence of steps in the legislative process varies slightly from state to state. Despite slight variations, however, all states generally conform to the information related to the legislative process provided in this *chapter. To be an effective lobbyist, you must obtain the legislative procedures of your own state and follow them.*

Summary

To become law, your bill must pass through a series of procedures prescribed by your state constitution and legislature. Legislative procedure is designed to be understood and you can follow the progress of your bill as it moves along the pathway.

You should work with your sponsor to control the amendments to your bill as much as possible. Managing your bill includes drafting it to minimize the number of committees who will review it, monitoring the actions of potentially interested parties, and attending sessions at which the bill may be amended.

You are now ready to enter the legislative arena. Here, you will find a main sponsor for your bill, secure co-sponsors, and learn to work with legislators, committees, and their staffs.

---

1 These rules are not laws; therefore the Governor does not and cannot approve them. Were the Governor's signature needed in order for the rules to become effective, a "separation of powers" constitutional problem would arise.

2 The Governor actively approves the bill by signing it into law. A formal ceremony may accompany his or her signing the bill. Passive approval may occur in states where a bill becomes law when the Governor fails to act on the bill within a given time period.

3 In instances when the legality of a proposal is at issue, the state attorney general or the legislature's legal counsel may have rendered an opinion on the legality of proposed legislation, the opinion may be reviewed by advocates in determining action to take on a bill.

4 Conservation of legislative resources has created several ways to streamline compliance with the three-readings rule. For example, in some jurisdictions bills placed on the consent calendar need not be read three times or publication in the chamber's journal may constitute the first reading. The three-readings rule may be divided by reading the bill twice in one body and once in the other.

5 Any member may object to a bill on first reading by raising the question to the chamber of whether the bill should be rejected. A bill may be rejected if its subject matter is inappropriate for legislative consideration or for procedural error. If the question is rejected, then the bill is referred to committee(s) for detailed consideration.

6 The presiding officer or Rules Committee assigns bills to committees.

7 These are called "joint," "double," or "multiple" referrals. In a joint referral, each committee is given jurisdiction over the bill. A referral may be sequential, in which case, one committee finishes with a bill and then sends it to another, and so on. The referral may be split, in which case, the bill is divided up among committees, each committee having jurisdiction over part of the bill.

8 A split referral may require two or more committees to find time meet together as a single group to consider the bill. This may be difficult to schedule. A sequential referral to too many committees promises that time will surely expire before all of them can consider the bill.

9 The bill normally goes to the Rules Committee before going to third reading. Various jurisdictions have different titles for the Rules Committee, such as Calendar Committee, Rules

and Calendar Committee, Committee on the Third Reading, Committee on Rules, or Joint Rules and Resolutions. The Rules Committee rules upon the constitutionality and legality of bills before the entire chamber considers the bill. It schedules the bill for second and third readings.

10 Some chambers do not use the Committee of the Whole. In a state, one chamber may use it and the sister chamber does not.

11 Yet, the bill concept may still become law. The bill is defeated as a stand-alone or free-standing bill. However, the language of the bill may in part or in whole become an amendment to another bill.

12 If both chambers pass companion bills, only one becomes law. The other bill stays in its house of origin where it dies upon adjournment of the session.

13 Generally, a local bill, a bill reported unanimously by a committee without amendment, or non-controversial bill is eligible for entry onto the consent calendar. In practice, unanimous consent works because it is requested only for non-controversial matters. Before the request is made, the chamber's members are advised and polled to make sure that there will be no objection. Bills on the consent calendar may not be amended.

14 For example, in one state the first regular session may consider any topic, while the second regular session is limited to Governor's legislation, legislation submitted by citizen initiative, emergency legislation, and legislation flowing from authorized studies.

15 For the legislature to call itself into session, a super majority of each house is required. During sessions called by the legislature, members may consider any matters they wish. During sessions called by the Governor the legislature may meet only to consider the items listed in the proclamation or those items added by a super majority of the legislature. Generally, there is no legal limit to the number of special sessions that may be called.

16 Committee recommendations for amendments are accepted almost all of the time. This is a major reason why your main lobbying goal will be to get a favorable recommendation out of the committee(s) of referral, especially the committee of first referral.

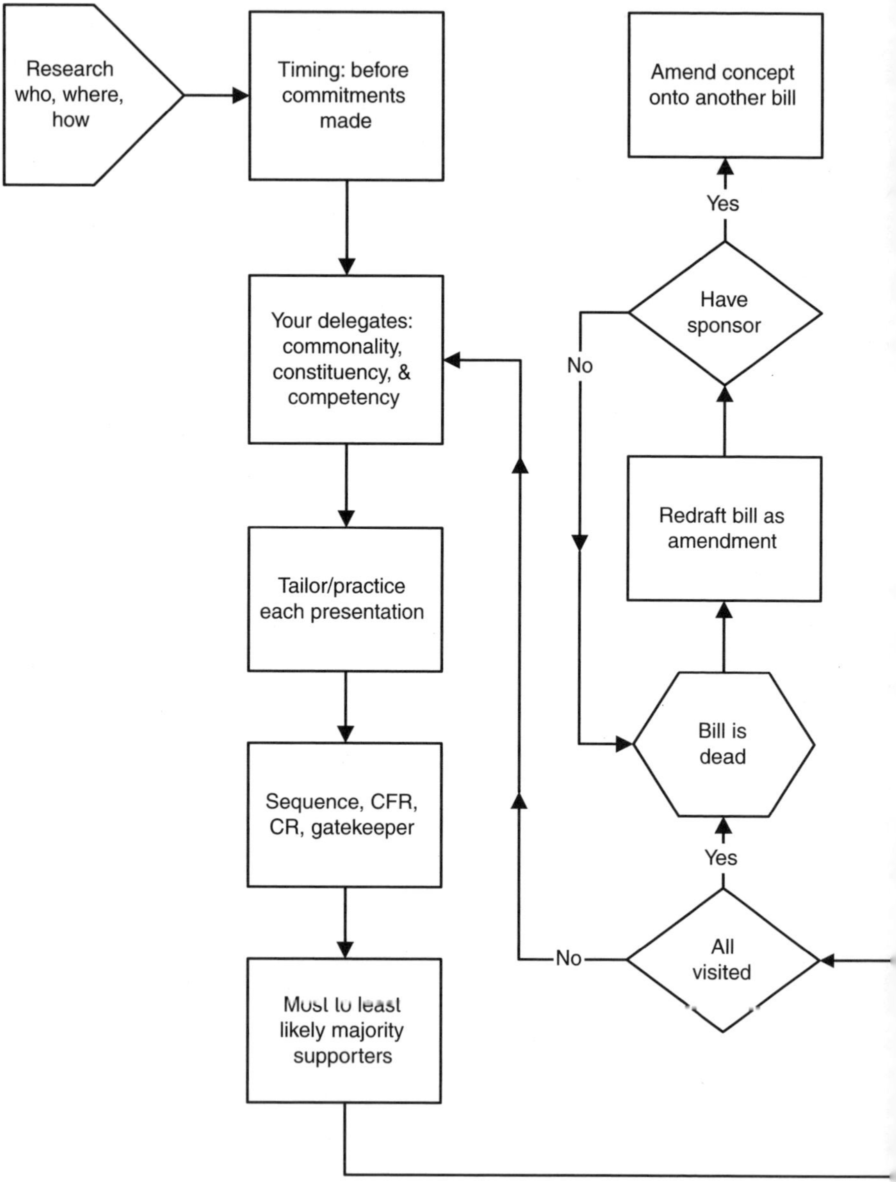
Research who, where, how
Timing: before commitments made
Your delegates: commonality, constituency, & competency
Tailor/practice each presentation
Sequence, CFR, CR, gatekeeper
Most to least likely majority supporters
Amend concept onto another bill
Yes
Have sponsor
No
Redraft bill as amendment
Bill is dead
Yes
All visited
No

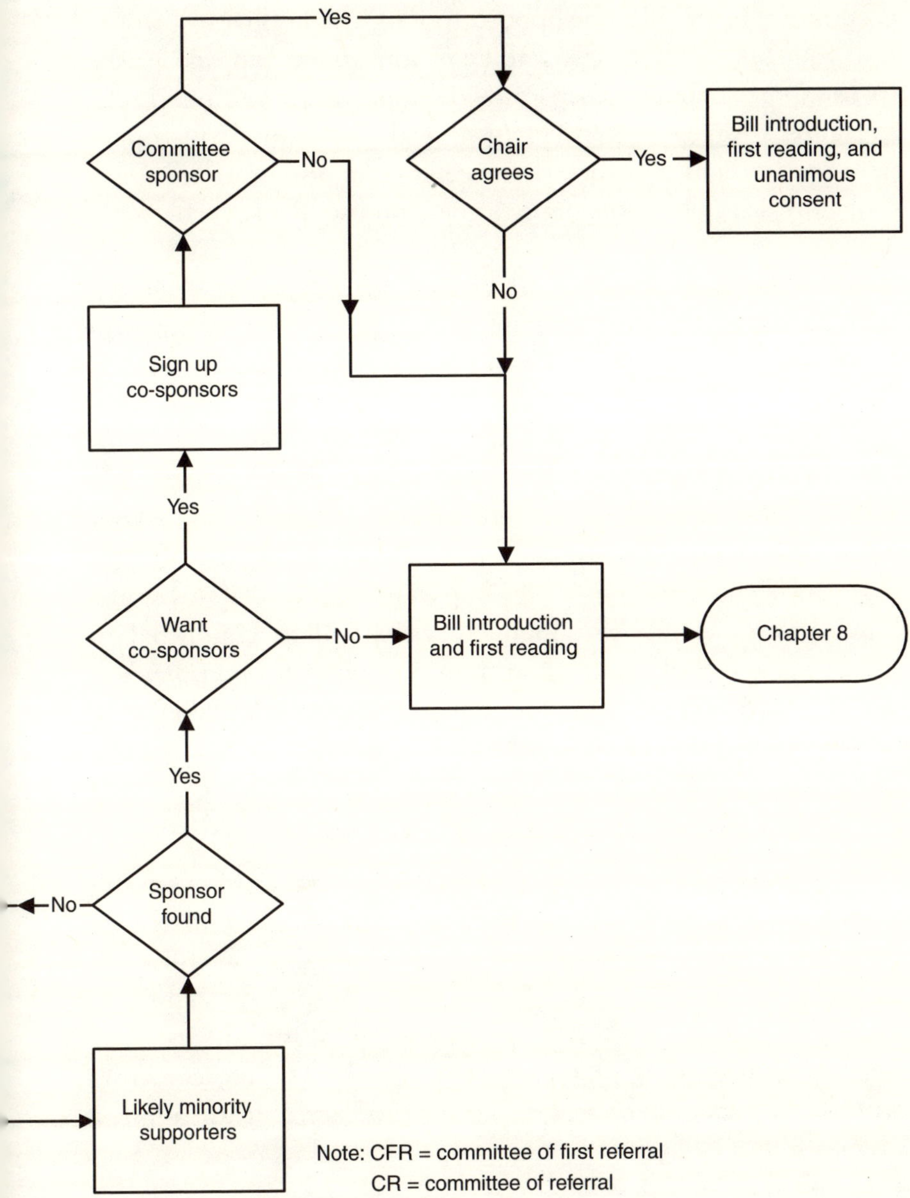

Note: CFR = committee of first referral
CR = committee of referral

The lobbying visit is the next activity in advancing your bill to enactment. It provides the opportunity for the Lobbying Team to find your bill's main sponsor, add co-sponsors, and engage legislative support. Lobbying visits provide opportunities to build relationships with lawmakers, predispose them against your opponents' views, and convince lawmakers to support your bill. Each lobbying visit follows the same format and uses the same mechanics.

Building relationships with elected officials is rewarding, relatively easy, and critical to your success. When a legislator supports you, he or she will work to advance and defend your interests in the capital. In the legislature, the lawmaker may sponsor, co-sponsor, or even lobby for your bill. As a member of the legislature, he or she has much greater access to "inside" information and can inform you about the internal activities surrounding your bill.

Once you have prepared your draft bill and, if necessary, hired a contract lobbyist, lobbying visits will be conducted to search for your bill's main sponsor and original co-sponsors. You will then garner support for your bill among other lawmakers supporting your issue and those who are undecided.

Lobbying to find the main sponsor

The relationship that you build with the main sponsor of your bill is the most important relationship that you will have with a legislator. He or she must be selected carefully because you will work so closely together. Sometimes called the *lead* sponsor, *patron,* or *author,* the main sponsor is most responsible for introducing your bill and managing its progress in the chamber. Other legislators will look to him or her for explanation, advocacy, and amendment of your bill.

Legislators invest time and energy to support bills that advance the interests of their districts and constituents, promote their party, and advance their own political views. They do not actively sponsor bills "just to be nice." Bill sponsorship requires the legislator and staff to spend time and political capital that could be dedicated to other matters.

As you seek your main sponsor, begin talking to candidates before they make commitments to sponsor other bills. This is especially important in states that restrict the number of bills that a lawmaker may sponsor during a session. You may begin your search as early as six months before the session begins.

Although all members of the chamber may be considered as candidates for your main sponsor, not all will be equally effective. An ideal main sponsor has these characteristics:

1. Membership in the majority party in the chamber
2. Membership on the committee of first referral or party leadership
3. Respect of other members of the chamber as a leader in issues dealing with the subject matter of your bill
4. Ability to learn your bill's subject matter
5. Enthusiasm for you and your issue

Information about prospective sponsors can be obtained from a number of sources including member data provided by the Clerk of the House or Secretary of the Senate, lobbyists, other legislators, and persons knowledgeable about state politics. Once you have obtained information about prospective sponsors, rank them in order of preference and probability that they would sponsor your bill. Then, personally interview those at the top of your list.

If you have some strong relationships with lawmakers who are supportive but would not meet these criteria, ask them to help you find a main sponsor. Not only can these friendly lawmakers suggest candidate sponsors, they may be willing to speak favorably on your behalf to fellow lawmakers.

Bring evidence of support for your bill from within the prospective sponsor's district to show the lawmaker how constituents and he or she will benefit from it. Bring important persons from the district, such as the mayor of a large city, to help reinforce the need for your bill. Finally, provide strong technical and policy arguments for your bill.

Invite a legislator to sponsor your bill if he or she has been ranked near the top of your list and appears supportive of you and your issue. If a candidate that you interview is interested but unable to sponsor your bill or seems clearly disinterested, then express gratitude for the time spent with you. Ask him or her to speak well of your bill to others and add that you hope to have his or her support when it comes time to vote on your issue. As much as possible, avoid being turned down in your request for sponsorship. A "no" that follows an invitation for sponsorship increases the likelihood that the next member on your list will also refuse. Most lawmakers will ask you to disclose the names of those candidates that you have also asked to sponsor your bill, and it is likely that they will tend to follow their lead.

If you find unanimous support for your bill among members of the committee of first referral, you might ask the chair to have the committee sponsor the bill. If he or she agrees, the bill will quickly move from first reading to the consent calendar.

Without a strong main sponsor, you must repackage your issue, accept a weaker main sponsor, or consider abandoning your project. If your bill is small, a sponsor not on the committee of first referral or in the minority party may be able to carry it if he or she has close supporters on the committee. If you have a strong relationship with leadership and the bill will not be difficult to carry, you could ask the leader to "assign" the bill to a junior lawmaker. With leadership's support for an easy bill, a junior legislator with unused bill allocations might welcome the opportunity for sponsorship.

Without a main sponsor, your bill cannot move forward. With a bad sponsor, your bill will usually be defeated so avoid sponsors who are unpopular or considered as extreme by the majority of the chamber.

You and the main sponsor will work closely together to advance your bill. Consequently, communicate regularly with him or her in order to solve problems, review strategy, and otherwise keep your bill moving.

Lobbying for co-sponsors

After enlisting your main sponsor, ask whether he or she would like to have *co-sponsors* on the bill. Since each bill usually has only one main sponsor, other legislators who wish to publicly support you may become co-sponsors. Generally, the more co-sponsors you have from each party, the greater the chance of bill enactment. Although any lawmaker can co-sponsor your bill, ideally, your co-sponsors will be drawn first from the committee(s) with jurisdiction over it.

Co-sponsors publicly place their names on your bill. If co-sponsors add their names *before* the bill is introduced in the chamber, they are called *original co-sponsors.* If added after the bill is introduced, they are simply called co-sponsors. Once original co-sponsors are secured, the main sponsor is ready to introduce your bill in accord with chamber procedures.

Lobbying other legislators

Now it is time to build support among the rest of the legislature for your bill. Start with the majority members of the committee of first referral. Plan carefully for each lobbying visit and design each one to maximize effectiveness and minimize expenditures of time, money, and political capital. With your main sponsor, identify those lawmakers with whom you will visit, plan when and where you will visit, and decide who will best represent your association to each lawmaker.

Research the political philosophies, voting records, party affiliations, and other published information about each legislator before the visit. Learn the characteristics of their constituents and the districts they represent to identify their most important concerns. Then, use these data to package and promote the relevant components of your issue to gain support for your bill.

Why will lawmakers listen to me?

Lawmakers want to hear from you for at least four reasons. First, they were elected to serve and advance the well-being of their electoral districts and its residents. If your bill affects the welfare of people living and working in their districts, they want to hear from you.

Second, elected representatives want to know the views of their constituents on the issues. Whenever possible, send constituents to visit their legislators to tell them why your bill has constituent benefit and support.

Third, each lawmaker seeks to advance his or her own political philosophy. Each was elected on a partisan political platform and will promote laws and public policy consistent with it. A lawmaker's political philosophy will lead him or her to join with either the supporters or opponents of your bill.

If an issue is neutral with regard to a legislator's philosophy, he or she will likely listen to your arguments for support. So, try to make your bill as personally and philosophically neutral as possible. Do not lose hope if your bill is weakly at odds with a lawmaker's philosophy. He or she may be willing to put aside small reservations about it if its enactment will serve most of the people in the district or if it brings him or her some political advantage.

Fourth, lawmakers need technical information in order to make good decisions about the issues that they face. Because they cannot follow the politics of every bill, they need information about other lawmakers and organizations that support and oppose you. They will appreciate facts, figures, and political information that they can rely upon.

Who to visit

You will face three groups of legislators as you lobby your issue: those who support you, those in opposition, and those who are undecided. Of these three, the largest group will be the undecided legislators to whom you will direct the greatest amount of your lobbying time and energy.

Prioritize visits to begin with likely supporters. These may be active or inactive; active supporters champion your issue publicly through words and actions whereas the inactive vote for your bill but are more concerned about other issues. Spend more time with active than inactive supporters.

Lobby the expected supportive majority party members followed by undecided majority party members on the committee of first referral. Then, lobby the committee chair. Finally, lobby the expected supporters followed by undecided members from the minority party on the committee of first referral. Repeat this procedure for all remaining committees of referral, if any.

Your final visits should include legislators who, although not appointed to committees of referral, support you and may even be willing to lobby fellow legislators and interest groups on behalf of your bill. These will be lawmakers with whom you have strong relationships.

If the opportunity to speak to chamber leaders arises, use it to advance your bill. However, since their focus is on administration and policy rather than the details of individual bills, their interest in your bill will likely be small unless it is very important to the chamber.

Do not visit lawmakers that you expect will strongly oppose you. Instead, send each one a letter that clearly describes why your bill is good for the state and for their constituents.

When to visit

To build a critical mass of legislative support, start visiting lawmakers as soon as you have a main sponsor. It will take time for you to explain your issue to a legislator or staff member and then elicit his or her support for your bill. Your goal is to meet with legislators before your opposition has had a chance to influence them. You also want to gain their support before other issues consume their attention.

During the session, the legislative calendars will show when legislators are available for lobbying in their home districts or in the capital. The calendars also show when lawmakers should be in committee, in full session, or in the office.

Where to visit

Visit lawmakers in places where you can get their attention: in their home districts, the state capital, social gatherings, conventions, and capitol hallways. The most common and appropriate places to meet with lawmakers are in their legislative offices at the state capital or in their legislative districts.

Lawmakers welcome contacts from the people in their electoral districts. However, when they are in their districts to meet with constituents, some may view appointments with non-constituents as unwelcome distractions. Consequently, if you have no constituent presence, inquire about a lawmaker's preference in meeting with non-constituents while in the district before you schedule a visit.

Some issues are important enough for lawmakers to travel outside of their electoral districts to visit with non-constituents. Important issues may be defined as those with widespread economic, social, or environmental impact upon the state or specific groups within the state. If your issue has statewide significance, invite lawmakers to your convention, place of business, or other location related to your issue. Inform the lawmakers representing your district that you have invited the guest lawmaker.

Making appointments

You should schedule appointments with lawmakers before the legislature goes into session, early in the session, or when there is in a lull in the session. Schedule as many different visits as possible for each day at thirty to sixty minute intervals. Provide each legislator's secretary with your lobbyists' and accompanying constituents' names, affiliation, and reason for the visit. A few days before the appointment date, confirm the meeting time and briefly reiterate what you plan to discuss.

Although scheduled appointments are preferred, during the session it is acceptable to simply "drop in" on legislators during office hours and ask for a brief moment to talk. Lawmakers and staff are in their offices to conduct the work of the people and meeting with the citizenry is one important component. Whether in or out of session, lawmakers and staff will try to make at least a few minutes available to you as they have the time.

Choosing your representatives

Choose two to four of the legislator's constituents from among your association members for the lobbying visit. Although any resident of the electoral district can be used to establish the lawmaker-constituent link, the most effective representative is a constituent who has a positive relationship with him or her. Select representatives who have as many characteristics as possible in common with the lawmaker. Appoint an articulate and credentialed member to serve as the spokesperson.

Your representatives should dress appropriately, but that does not necessarily mean formally. If your attire would send a positive message, such as is found in distinctive work clothes or uniforms, then more than one of you should wear them.

If you hire a contract lobbyist, include him or her in the visit if he or she has a good relationship with the lawmaker. If no relationship exists, bring a constituent rather than the lobbyist. Exclude anyone, association member or contract lobbyist, from your meeting if he or she has a poor relationship with the lawmaker.

If a committee chair, chamber leader, or "swing vote" member's support will be critical for your bill, bring a prestigious person from his or her district who has a positive or neutral relationship with the lawmaker. Persons to consider include the leaders of important companies, public interest groups, unions, or local government. The presence of a community leader communicates the importance of your issue, the district's need for the lawmaker's support, and suggests a likely political benefit to the lawmaker.

If you cannot locate an available constituent for the visit, inform the lawmaker that although not present, his or her constituents are part of your group. Mention their names and affiliations following careful research to ensure that the lawmaker has no negative relationships with any of them. If no constituents are part of your association, try to find some or make the visit without them.

Your formal presentation

Your presentation should show why your bill is good public policy with benefit to the lawmaker's district. Plan each word. Your case will be won or lost in the first few minutes of the presentation. The three most important elements of the presentation are:

1. The names of the main sponsor, co-sponsors, and other legislators who support it
2. The names of constituents, important persons, and associations who support you or your bill
3. The factual bases for your bill. The Drafting Team will have already prepared the factual support for the bill.

Remember that most lawmakers and staff are lay persons who likely know little about your issue. Make your presentation simple, especially if the issue is highly technical or complex. As non-experts, technical subtleties and explanations can be very difficult for legislators and their staff to understand. Use visual aids, exhibits, story telling, and analogies to engage the listeners. Make the presentation interesting and relevant to the lawmaker's philosophy and district. Practice until you are comfortable and can convey the merits of your bill with confidence.

Provide a list of supporters, starting with lawmakers who share his or her philosophy or party affiliation. Then, list the names of organizations, interest groups, influential constituents, and other individuals who support your bill. This political information will be central to helping the lawmaker decide his or her likely position on your bill.

Every chamber usually has a member respected for expertise in an area of knowledge. Make a special effort to gain his or her support. Legislators look to these fellow legislators for guidance. Commonly, a lawmaker may conclude, "If Legislator ___ supports the bill, then I can be sure it is a good bill."

When preparing your factual presentation, anticipate the lawmaker's interests and position on your bill. Determine how you will reinforce favorable views, rebut opposing positions, and answer the questions that he or she might ask. In passing, mention the contacts you have had with bill opponents. This disclosure is necessary to affirm your honesty and trustworthiness to the lawmaker. It also provides him or her with important political information.

Do not speak negatively about anyone, even if the comments are true. Rebut arguments but never defame a person. Negative comments undermine the speaker as well as the one being defamed.

In light of the thousands of bills introduced into the legislature each session, legislators and staff have limited time to give to you and your issue. This is especially true during the height of the legislative session. Your presentation should be concise and take ten minutes or less. Do not irritate your listeners by taking too much time. The lawmaker or staff will listen to a well prepared presentation and, if interested, will ask you for more time and information. Your schedule will enable you to give the interested lawmaker more time because you have scheduled your next appointment thirty to sixty minutes from this one. Make sure, however, that you call your next appointment and adjust the meeting time if you are going to be late.

The visit

After the initial introductions have been made, you should express gratitude to the lawmaker and staff for their efforts on behalf of constituents. Then, begin the prepared formal presentation. Be sensitive to notice when the legislator or staff wants to speak. At regular intervals in the presentation, pause for input and comments. The team members should listen closely to what the legislator or staff says, observe how the message is received, take notes about the visit, and provide supporting comments, as appropriate.

If the "mood" of the visit is good, ask the legislator if you can count on his or her vote. If strong support is expressed, ask him or her to recommend your bill to undecided party members who serve on the committee(s) of referral. A lawmaker who speaks on your behalf to a fellow legislator on a committee of referral might gain support that would be otherwise unattainable.

If the legislator does not commit, state you understand that more facts or time may be needed to enable a decision about your bill. Communicate your interest in assisting the legislator and his or her staff with information.

As the visit concludes, leave a one page summary sheet. You may attach it to more detailed but limited supporting information. While gift giving is not recommended, inexpensive tokens such as a pen, coffee mug, T-shirt, or other low cost items representing your issue and given to all legislators may help him or her recall your bill. However, before you leave these physical reminders you must be sure you comply with the legislature's gift rules on what you can offer or what the legislator may accept.

Be sure to thank the legislator or staff person for the visit and follow up with a written thank you letter to the lawmaker. Send a photocopy of the letter to the individual staff members and be sure to include a handwritten note of personal thanks to each of them.

Try to build future contacts into the visit because you are competing with hundreds of others for the lawmaker's attention. Offer to send additional information and, after sending it, call to ensure that it has been received. During the call, ask if the legislator or staff have additional questions about your issue. The more contacts you make, the more opportunity you have to reinforce your position with the lawmaker and staff.

Follow-up visits

Short follow-up visits should be made to supportive and still undecided legislators immediately before they vote on your bill. These visits, along with grass roots lobbying from the district, help preserve the supportive lawmakers' commitments to you and help the undecided resist the opposition who will be working to discourage their support of you.

Although the passage of your bill by the committee(s) of referral is critical to your bill's success, do not forget that the entire chamber votes on your bill one or more times. When the full chamber is about to consider your bill, lobby those legislators who you believe might be willing to speak from the floor on your behalf. These may be members of committee(s) of referral or members whose districts will be positively affected by your bill becoming law.

Remember these points

Tell your lobbyist(s) and representatives that they do not have the authority to "commit" the association to a position. As you visit lawmakers, some may ask you to agree to amend the bill. You should inform legislators that you do not have the authority to commit your association to any legislative position. However, tell them that their request will be passed on to the association for action. When you bring back the association's reply, this will provide yet another opportunity to lobby lawmakers.

Never offer the lawmaker your opinions as to what his or her support or opposition to your bill will mean politically. Any suggestions that failure to support your bill will harm or help him or her at election time is wholly out of order and may be taken as a threat. Lawmakers calculate the political consequences of their actions.

Do not give legislators special gifts. Do not offer campaign contributions. Do not offer political support. Let everything you do relate solely to constituent interest in the bill and the facts that support its passage.

After your presentation, you may find that a lawmaker who seemingly supports you refuses to commit his or her vote to your bill. This does not mean that he or she opposes you, rather, some lawmakers keep their options open and are silent for political reasons until the vote is called. A very few do not come to a decision until the moment of the vote.

If you find that a lawmaker does not support you, do not be discouraged. A lawmaker's lack of support may result from forces wholly unrelated to your bill. Remember that you only need the votes from the majority of lawmakers. You do not need them all.

Occasionally, despite a commitment to you, a lawmaker may withdraw support. Remember that neither you nor your opponents truly have a lawmaker's vote until it is cast. This is why you must remain in contact with supportive and undecided lawmakers.

Finally, do not be disappointed if a lawmaker's staff person, rather than the legislator, meets with you. If a legislator is not able to give you personal attention, the fact that he or she sends a staff person to meet with you should be taken as a sign of interest. Treat the staff person with the same respect and deference that you would show the legislator.

Remain gracious throughout the lobbying process. You want to leave legislators with a good impression of you and your association. Do not forget, you may be back next year.

Lobbying legislative staff[1]

Lawmakers rely on their staff and spend large amounts of time working closely with them. The staff manage the lawmakers' personal offices and provide chamber support services. They give legal counsel, technical advice, and recommendations to lawmakers on a variety of possible legislative actions. The staff have tremendous influence on the direction the legislature takes regarding your bill.

The staff provide you with opportunities to affect the direction of your bill. For issues that the legislator wishes to move forward, he or she asks staff to research the issue and provide the supporting data needed to convince others to vote for a favored bill. For other issues, legislators ask their staff to research the issue and advise them how to vote. Similarly, committees rely on staff to provide subject matter expertise, legal counsel, and analyses of the economic, social, environmental, and other impacts of proposed legislation.

The staff want to do a good job, but like the legislators they work for, they suffer from the same excessive workloads, inadequate amounts of time in the session, and shortage of resources. Because they are dedicated and highly motivated, they are interested in receiving the facts, figures, data, and supporting information about your bill. Educate the staff about your bill to help them make good recommendations to the legislators.

While both junior and senior staff serve in the legislature, the senior staff are most important to you because they serve in leadership positions. Their many years of experience within the legislature have given them technical knowledge, insights to fine points of chamber procedures, and institutional memory. They are the most influential staff members in the legislature. You may interact with four different categories of staff.

Personal staff

A lawmaker may have one or more personal staff. These aides help the lawmaker with his or her particular legislative duties. The lawmaker's district office staff focus on communicating with constituents and meeting their needs. Capital office staff conduct research, develop policy, draft bills, and provide technical analyses. Some lawmakers delegate authority to speak on their behalf to their personal staff.

Committee staff

A committee may have its own staff comprised of clerical and technical persons. Clerical staff record the meetings, keep the minutes, receive written testimony and other submittals, distribute meeting packets, and provide general support functions. Technical staff have expertise in the subject matter and legal considerations of matters within the committee's jurisdiction. Most lawmakers seldom understand the fine points of technical matters for subjects reviewed by the committees to which they are assigned. Therefore, many rely heavily on the technical guidance of the staff.

Chamber staff

The chamber employs a Clerk or Secretary, Sergeant-at-Arms, and their assistants. The chamber staff perform clerical functions, maintain order in the chamber, and complete other related duties. Computer support services, the bill room, and a host of other offices are managed to enable the chamber to operate smoothly. You will be in regular contact with chamber staff.

Legislative services agencies' staff

Unlike members of the personal, committee, and chamber staff who are political appointees, legislatures have non-partisan offices to assist members and the chamber in technical matters. For example, the Office of Legislative Counsel assists lawmakers as they draft bills and assures that all bills are procedurally and legally correct. Other non-partisan offices of the legislature report objectively on the likely economic, environmental, social, and other impacts of proposed legislation. Although it is unlikely that you will work with them, your sponsor could request that you meet with these staff to explain your bill.

Treat all staff with the greatest respect. There are no unimportant staff. Ask any lobbyist who has failed to persuade a Doorkeeper to bring a message to a lawmaker on the floor or has failed to meet with a legislator because the secretary "just could not fit the appointment in" what he or she will do differently in the future.

Summary

By learning to work with legislators and their staff, you will be more successful in the legislature. Most legislators on committees of referral, the committee staff, and a lawmaker's personal staff are interested in learning about your issue and will listen carefully to your arguments. A concise and politically powerful presentation will enable you to secure a main sponsor, add co-sponsors, and persuade other legislators to support you. Once you have gained sufficient support, you must maintain it throughout the voting process. By working with staff, you can capitalize on major opportunities to gain support for your bill. Gaining a favorable recommendation from the committee of first referral and other committees of referral, if any, are the next critical steps in securing the success of your bill.

---

1 Staffing levels vary among the states. These levels range from no personal staff to having several full time personal staff; from having one part-time committee clerical staff to having several full time clerical and professional staff.

8 Working with Legislative Committees

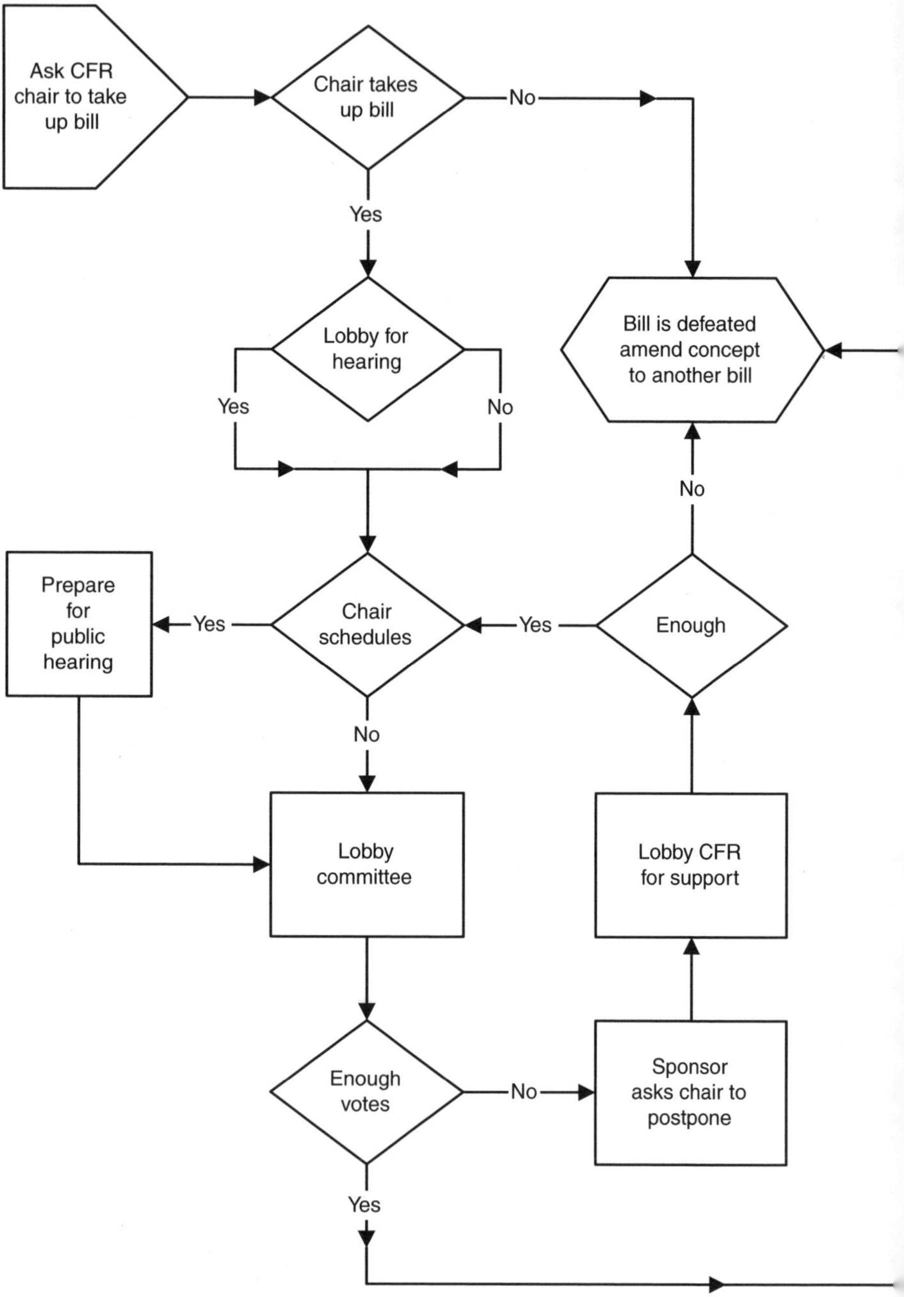

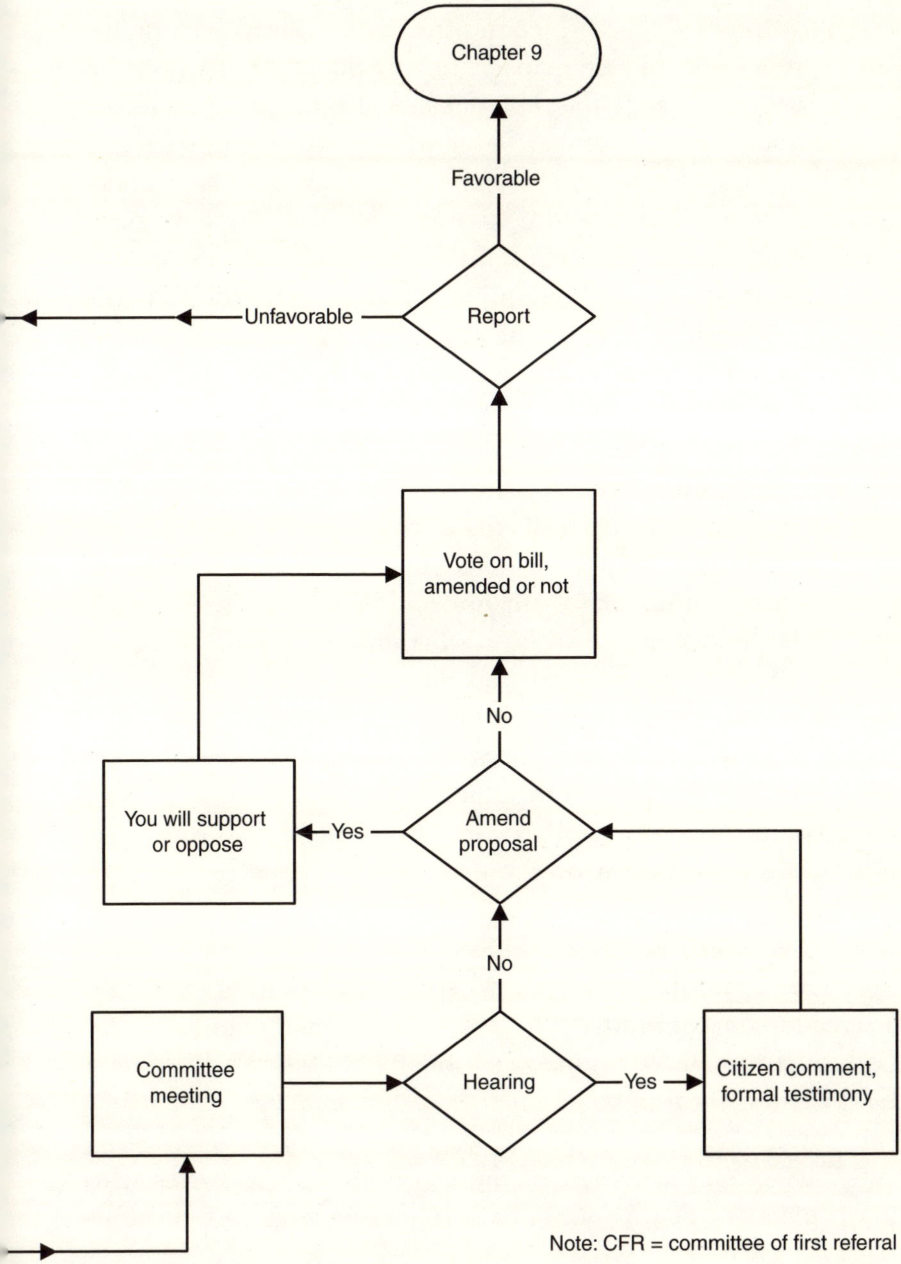

Note: CFR = committee of first referral

The committee system has been called "the factory floor of the legislative process" because committees accomplish most of the legislature's work. To help manage their workload, legislators form committees and divide the thousands of bills proposed each year among them. Each chamber develops its own committees and each committee has its exclusive areas of jurisdiction. A chamber may have more than one dozen committees and these, in turn, may have one or more subcommittees.

The membership of committees is usually proportional to the party membership in each chamber. The party caucus recommends each lawmaker to the President or Speaker for appointment to membership on those committees in which the legislator has expressed an interest. The Speaker or President is then responsible for appointing members from both parties to committees and committee chairs from the majority party.

The Speaker or President refers bills to committees that are charged with considering them in detail. The committee of first referral is the committee with jurisdiction over the main subject matter of your bill. A bill must pass through the committee of first referral in order to proceed to subsequent committees, if any, and to votes by the full chamber. Committees limit their consideration to aspects of the bill within their authority and they do not review the recommendations of other committees of referral. Any committee with jurisdiction over your bill may amend or defeat it. Therefore, it is important to lobby the members and staff of all committees considering your bill to gain favorable action.

The committee chair decides the direction of each bill assigned to the committee. This may include whether or not it will be brought up in committee; if brought up, whether or not to hold a public hearing; and whether or not to assign it to a subcommittee.

The recommendation of the committee of first referral to pass, amend, or defeat your bill determines, in large part, its probability of enactment. This is because the chamber usually implements committee recommendations. Inaction or an unfavorable report will usually defeat your bill. So, your challenge is to gain favorable committee action on your bill.

Gaining favorable committee action

The Lobbying Team should learn the practice of the legislature and its committees regarding consideration of bills. You must know whether all bills are referred automatically to committees, and if not, how you will ensure that your bill will be referred. Usually, all bills are referred.

In some states, committees automatically consider all referred bills while in others this is the decision of the chair. There may be several reasons that the chair does not bring your bill before the committee: it may consume excessive amounts of committee time; it may not be likely to pass; it may be too unimportant relative to other bills; or there may be political reasons. When consideration of a referred bill occurs at the chair's discretion, you should lobby him or her to take it up even before your bill is assigned to the expected committee of first referral.

Before you ask the chair to take up your bill for committee consideration, you and your sponsor must discuss the advisability of having a *public hearing,* often also called a *committee hearing.* If a public hearing is held at the chair's discretion, you may want to ask for one when you ask him or her to take up your bill. Although the committee must consider your bill in order for it to become law, you do not necessarily need to have the public comment on it.

If a hearing would delay bill progress or you do not want to give your opponents an opportunity to enter negative comments into the committee report, you may not want the chair to hold a hearing. On the other hand, a public hearing might be a great opportunity to make your case to the committee and have your supporters display public support. In some states, public comment is automatically taken.

Whether the chair holds or does not hold a public hearing, you should offer technical assistance to committee staff to ensure that they use the correct data in formulating their analyses and developing recommendations for the committee. Information and assistance from you and your technical experts may result in reports to your benefit.

Public hearing

Despite your wishes, the chair may choose to hold a public hearing if your bill impacts state government, the public, state policy, or is controversial enough that committee deliberations will benefit from citizen perspectives on all sides of the issue. On the other hand, if your bill appears to have wide committee support, the chair may conclude that holding a public hearing will waste the time of the committee and the public. If the chair decides to invite the public to express its views on your bill, a portion of the committee meeting to consider your bill will be dedicated to receiving public comment. This will be the only formal opportunity that supporters and opponents will have to present the committee with their positions on your bill.

The chair may allow the public to express its views to the committee through formal testimony, citizen comment, or both. In formal testimony, the chair invites a few persons closely identified with the bill to give formal presentations. During citizen comment, all other persons attending the committee meeting may speak about the bill. The chair may choose to have formal testimony but no citizen comment, formal testimony followed by citizen comment, or no formal testimony but allow citizen comment. The chair must also decide when the hearing will occur, the length of time needed for the hearing, and whether to have the full committee or a subcommittee consider the bill and hold the hearing.

The taking of formal testimony usually occurs in the committee of first referral. Since each chamber has its own committee of first referral, each chamber may hold a public hearing on your bill. However, in practice, if one chamber holds a formal hearing on your bill the other normally does not duplicate efforts by holding its own hearing, unless each party controls one chamber in a partisan legislature. Further, any committee considering your bill may ask for citizen comment on the portion of the bill over which it has jurisdiction, and if testimony is given to a subcommittee, it will not be given again to the full committee.

Because you may appear before one or more legislative committees or subcommittees to explain your bill, you should maintain communication with your bill's sponsor, the chairs of the committees to consider your bill, and their staffs. Even before the chair of the committee of first referral has decided to schedule a hearing, tell him or her that you would like to testify if a hearing is held. Once the hearing has been scheduled, immediately remind the chair and clerk or chief committee staff person that you would like to testify.

Notice of committee hearing

Most public hearings by the committee of first referral take place during pre-session or early in the session and are announced well in advance. A committee chair generally keeps a planning calendar that shows when certain bills might be heard. Contact committee staff regularly to inquire about when your bill will be heard. As a matter of courtesy in some states and as a matter of course in others, a bill's main sponsor is notified in advance of a hearing. Thus, you should ask your sponsor to notify you about a hearing on your bill as soon as the chair notifies him or her. It may be possible, however, that neither the sponsor nor you will know about the hearing until a few days before it is scheduled to occur. For this reason, have your testimony ready to be given at any time.

Preparing for the committee meeting and hearing —

Prior to the committee meeting in which your bill will be considered, you should meet with all committee members expected to support you or who could be convinced to support you. If a few weeks have elapsed since your last contacts, meet briefly with committee members to update them about the progress of your bill. Starting a few days before the committee meeting, ask constituents of each committee member to send letters or make calls urging a favorable vote on your bill.

The preparations for formal testimony and citizen comment are similar. For formal testimony, update and revise the written and oral committee testimony developed by the Drafting Team prior to bill introduction. In addition to being factual, informative, and well researched, your committee testimony should convey the message that your goal is to help the legislators reach a good decision on a good idea, that is, your proposed bill. Your bill should advance the public good and its presentation must be succinct and focused. Use a bit of human interest to say why you care and why they should care about your issue.

In your written formal testimony, include legislative developments that have occurred since bill introduction, information about similar bills and proposed executive agency rules, names of co-sponsors, the other chamber's response to your bill, amendments, current estimates of fiscal and other impacts, and names of new supporters. Inform the committee of any positions taken by executive agencies, such as the Governor's office or administrative departments on your bill and briefly mention those who oppose you. Mention similar actions in other states and emphasize actions by bell-wether or precedent setting legislatures. Condense the formal testimony into oral testimony and prepare a short written summary of your oral comments.

Before the committee hearing, determine how many copies of written testimony and summary of oral testimony to provide. Expect to give one copy to each committee member and the committee secretary and distribute additional copies to staff. Find out when your materials should be delivered. Ask if exhibits may be brought to the public hearing and ask if a helper may accompany you to aid your presentation.

Discover the conventions for testifying before the committee. For example, how are committee members to be addressed? In some states, the address is quite formal with seemingly every sentence preceded by, "Honorable Chair X and members of the Committee Y." Other states are less formal. Determine if a formal witness registration card must be submitted to the committee clerk prior to your testimony.

Ask the staff to estimate the length of time for the committee meeting, the amount of time that will be given to the formal testimony and citizen comments on your bill, the amount of time that you will have to speak, the percentage of time you should allocate to your formal presentation, and the percentage of time to allow for questions. Usually, the time allocated for formal testimony is short and ranges from several minutes per speaker in the committee of first referral to a minute or less in successive committees. Ask the staff for the names of others invited to testify about your bill and learn whether the committee members will ask questions. Anticipate the objections of your opponents as you redraft your testimony. Ask for the names of other bills likely to be considered at the same meeting, estimate the time given to these other bills, and determine if any of them are controversial. Ask for your bill to be considered early on the agenda so that you will not lose time to other bills that may require more time than expected.

In preparation for the committee meeting, the committee staff prepare bill analyses, fact-sheets, and other technical documents for committee members and the public. The legislative services agency may additionally provide analyses of economic, environmental, social, and state budget impacts. Amendments may have been filed with the committee secretary. The agenda for the public hearing, sign-in cards, staff-prepared materials, copies of bills to be considered, and proposed amendments are all available prior to the meeting. The agenda will include lists of bills to be considered, the sequence of consideration, and the time allocated for bill deliberation. Ask the staff to give you copies of these documents.

Use all of the time you have been allocated for your oral presentation. Plan every moment of your time before the committee. Remember that your bill will likely be one of several considered during a meeting. Depending on where your bill is scheduled on the agenda and how well the chair manages time, even a well-prepared presentation may find itself in a race with time. Prepare a shortened version of your testimony in case your time is unexpectedly cut short.

Your representative who gives formal testimony at the hearing should be a person who speaks well, understands the issues, and can calmly and succinctly answers legislators' questions, even hostile ones. Ideally, he or she will have an impressive title and credentials such as president or officer of your organization or recognized expert on the topic. If your representative does not have the required credentials or needs technical assistance, ask a member of your association or consultant who is credentialed to accompany him or her.

Your representative must be prepared to answer any challenges to his or her compliance with state lobbying laws, especially registration. Failure to conform to state lobbyist registration requirements can lead to a variety of actions that range from public embarrassment, to being forced to sit down, and possible enforcement action by the state.

You should now authorize your representative to bind your organization in agreements if moved by an offer or forced into one that seems beneficial to the association. This is the opposite of earlier instruction where you intentionally denied authority to commit to your representatives and lobbyists. Now, if you do not give your representative the authority to commit, he or she and your association become irrelevant to the amendment process and the amendments to your bill will go forward without your input.

Because your bill's sponsor will also testify at the hearing, you must coordinate your two testimonies. They must be harmonious presentations that support each other and do not present conflicting messages. Reinforce one another from different perspectives to appeal to the broad audience of legislators.

As soon as the agenda for the meeting is published, study it to assess the appropriateness of your planned presentation and testimony. Locate the room in which the hearing will be held and note the room number and seating capacity. Because anyone may attend a committee meeting, you can make your presence more strongly known by filling the committee room with your supporters. If the room is small, prepare to have your supporters arrive early to ensure their seating. Instruct them about decorum, coordinate what each might say, and if citizen comments are to be taken, the appropriate way to speak to the committee.

Shortly before the hearing, you should be able to estimate the number of votes that will be cast for and against your bill. There may be one or two votes that are not known, but you must have a good idea as to whether or not the committee will vote to support your bill. If you think that the vote will not be favorable, then discuss other strategies with your sponsor. For example, should he or she request that the committee chair postpone consideration of your bill? Although delay is bad, defeat is far worse.

The committee meeting and public hearing

As the committee meeting is about to begin, you may find that the lack of a quorum threatens the meeting and, therefore, committee consideration of your bill. Rather than lose your opportunity, ask the chair to designate those members in attendance as a special temporary subcommittee. This subcommittee would have its required quorum and could proceed with a subcommittee meeting, take testimony, make recommendations for amendments, and issue a report to the full committee for action. If the chair agrees, the subcommittee meeting and your public hearing will proceed.

Before the committee meeting, you should provide the committee secretary with the correct number of copies of written testimony and summary of the oral presentation. Inform the secretary that you will refer to these documents during your presentation.

Bill consideration normally begins with discussion of the materials prepared by the legislative services agency staff and committee staff. The materials include an explanation of the bill and expected fiscal and other impacts. Next, the sponsor of the bill testifies about the merits of the bill, often explains it section-by-section, and answers committee members' questions. He or she may bring others to assist or otherwise help make the case. Formal testimony will be taken after the committee finishes with the sponsor.

For formal testimony, one or more panels of advocates and opponents, often including representatives of affected government agencies, speak to the bill. Each makes his or her presentation until all invited speakers have spoken.

As you begin your testimony, inform the committee that your written testimony and its summary have been given to the secretary. It is likely that he or she has already given a copy to each lawmaker. If you bring an expert to assist you, announce the name and credentials of that person and state that he or she is there to answer members' technical questions. Stay within the allotted time for your oral testimony and you will be allowed to complete it without interruption. When you finish your testimony, thank the chair and the committee for allowing you to speak. The chair may allow committee members to question you about the bill and your statements or will ask them to hold their questions until later.

At the conclusion of formal presentations, the chair may invite citizen comments on your bill. Before speaking, make sure that you and your supporters have met the speaker's registration requirements, if any. Some states do not recognize a person wishing to speak to a bill unless, prior to the meeting, he or she has submitted a registration card to the committee secretary. The card asks for the speaker's name, affiliation, and pro or con position on the bill.

Except for adherence to time limits, and perhaps a requirement for speaker registration, the comment period is open to all relevant remarks. Several formats may be used. The most common is one in which citizens simply go the microphone, state their names, indicate who they represent, and disclose their views about a bill. An alternate format is for the chair to call persons to speak in the order in which they submitted their registration cards to the secretary. The chair may also separate proponents from opponents and ask the proponents to speak first. If comments become redundant, the chair may then ask subsequent speakers to limit comments to the provision of new information.

After formal testimony and during citizen comment, the chair may allow committee members to ask you questions. If you do not know the answer to a question, just say so, promise to find the answer, and get back to the committee member and other members promptly. This presents another lobbying opportunity. Never respond with hostility to unfriendly questions from committee members because they are seldom personal attacks. You should always maintain composure and diplomacy.

After closing the public hearing, the chair will resume committee deliberations by asking the committee for advice about the action to take on your bill. In the committee of first referral your sponsor, if a member, will make a motion or *move* for adoption of the bill. If your bill is sent to subsequent committees of referral or if your sponsor is not on the committee of first referral, then you and your sponsor must find a supportive committee member to make that motion and otherwise champion your bill. The chair will then allow the committee discussion to take its course during which amendments may be proposed.

Dealing with proposed amendments

Expect that amendments to your bill will be proposed during committee consideration. Those who oppose you will try to amend your bill unfavorably, hoping to defeat it. Others, including those previously interested in your bill, may try to amend their issue onto your bill to keep it moving forward. Other committee members may propose amendments to make the bill more acceptable or better.

Prior to the proposal of an amendment by a legislator on the committee, expect that someone will ask you to agree to amend your bill. Your agreement or opposition to an amendment may greatly affect the likelihood of committee adoption. This may occur before or during the committee meeting. In the meeting itself, a legislator may pressure you to agree to changes. He or she may state that the bill has a significant problem that must be resolved by the involved parties before the committee vote is taken. You may find yourself negotiating amendments in the hallway during a short committee recess.

You should *agree* to support a proposed amendment if it:

1. Is reasonable
2. Does not harm your goals
3. Increases the probability of bill passage
4. Will be sponsored by a powerful committee member
5. Receives your sponsor's support
6. Will not be defeated by a majority of votes in committee

You should *disagree* with a proposed amendment if it:

1. Is unreasonable
2. Would harm your goals
3. Would decrease the likelihood of bill passage
4. Is sponsored by a group not supported by a majority of the committee
5. Is championed by a weak sponsor
6. Is opposed by your sponsor
7. Will be defeated by a majority of votes in committee

Most likely, amendments will be proposed whether you agree to them or not. Remember, the bill belongs to the legislature, not to you, and the committee can do anything it wants to the bill. However, if the amendment sponsor states that you agree with the proposed changes, your supporters on the committee will likely vote for the amendment. On the other hand, when a supportive committee member reports that you oppose the amendment, your supporters are more likely to oppose it, too.

Committee action

Each amendment is voted on individually by voice vote. After all amendments have been considered, discussion is closed and the chair allows a motion and vote to report the bill, as amended or not. This is normally a roll call vote. The chair then announces the decision of the committee. A committee may take several actions:

1. Report a bill favorably
2. Report an amended bill favorably
3. Report a bill amended so extensively by the committee that it becomes a substitute for the original bill. In some jurisdictions the substitute bill may be called a committee substitute (CS) for the original bill, for example CS/HB ___. Other jurisdictions do not indicate when substitutions occur.
4. Take no action
5. Vote not to report a bill out of committee
6. Take some intermediate action, such as *temporarily passing* or *tabling* the bill, actions that effectively defeat it
7. Report the bill without recommendation
8. Report an amended bill without recommendation
9. Report the bill, but recommend it be referred to a different committee
10. Report the bill unfavorably

The first action above is good for your bill because committee approval will help move it toward passage. The second action is good for the amended bill and hopefully will not adversely affect your needs or lead to losing the bill in second reading. The third action may indicate that another bill has replaced your bill and that your bill is defeated. When actions one, two, or three occur by unanimous committee vote, the bill may be sent to the consent calendar for final vote by the chamber. The other actions probably indicate that your bill is defeated

After the committee meeting, thank each committee member for giving consideration to your bill, whether he or she voted for or against it. If the vote was favorable, you now need to prepare for subsequent committee meetings, if any, or for second reading. If it was unfavorable, meet with your main sponsor to determine the next step. Your most likely action will be to try to amend your concept onto a bill that is moving forward in one or both chambers.

Parliamentary procedures, such as a motion to discharge a committee from consideration of the bill, can help revive a stalled or unfavorably reported bill. However, given the limited amount of time and chamber's deference to committee recommendations, in practice, most rescue actions fail. Your sponsor will advise you of the chance for a successful rescue of your bill.

Do not forget that after your bill passes the committee of first referral, other committees may also consider it, although in a much more limited sense. Your bill may be stalled, defeated, or amended in these committees. While unlikely that you will give formal testimony again, you must communicate with all committees and attend all committee meetings in which your bill is considered.

The committee report and second reading

The committee will issue a formal report of its findings and recommendations to the chamber. The report may include a listing of the roll call vote(s), a detailed bill analysis, a memorandum explaining the committee's view of the bill and its recommendations, and general information such as the testimony. The clerk, secretary, or chamber legal counsel uses this report to prepare a revised bill for distribution at second or third reading.

After all committees have considered your bill, the Committee of the Whole considers the report of the committee of first referral. It will usually implement the committee's recommendations. With a favorable report, the chamber will likely pass the bill at second reading, amended or not, calendar it and move it to third reading. However, passage is not certain even with a favorable report. You must attend the readings to deal with proposed amendments, votes on your bill, or excessive delay.

Summary

In order to become law, your bill must secure approvals from one or more committees. Approval by the committee of first referral gives a huge boost to your bill as it moves through a chamber. However, if other committees consider your bill, you must ensure that they pass it, too. If your bill receives a public hearing you will want to prepare to make a strong case for passage. Your bill must secure every approval and avoid unfavorable amendments in order to achieve your legislative goals. Should your bill falter you may be able to rescue your issue by amending it onto a bill that is likely to become law.

After the committee meeting(s), you must prepare for the second and third readings and votes. These will be followed by the other chamber's actions on your bill and hopefully, enrollment.

9 Activities: Now and Post-Session

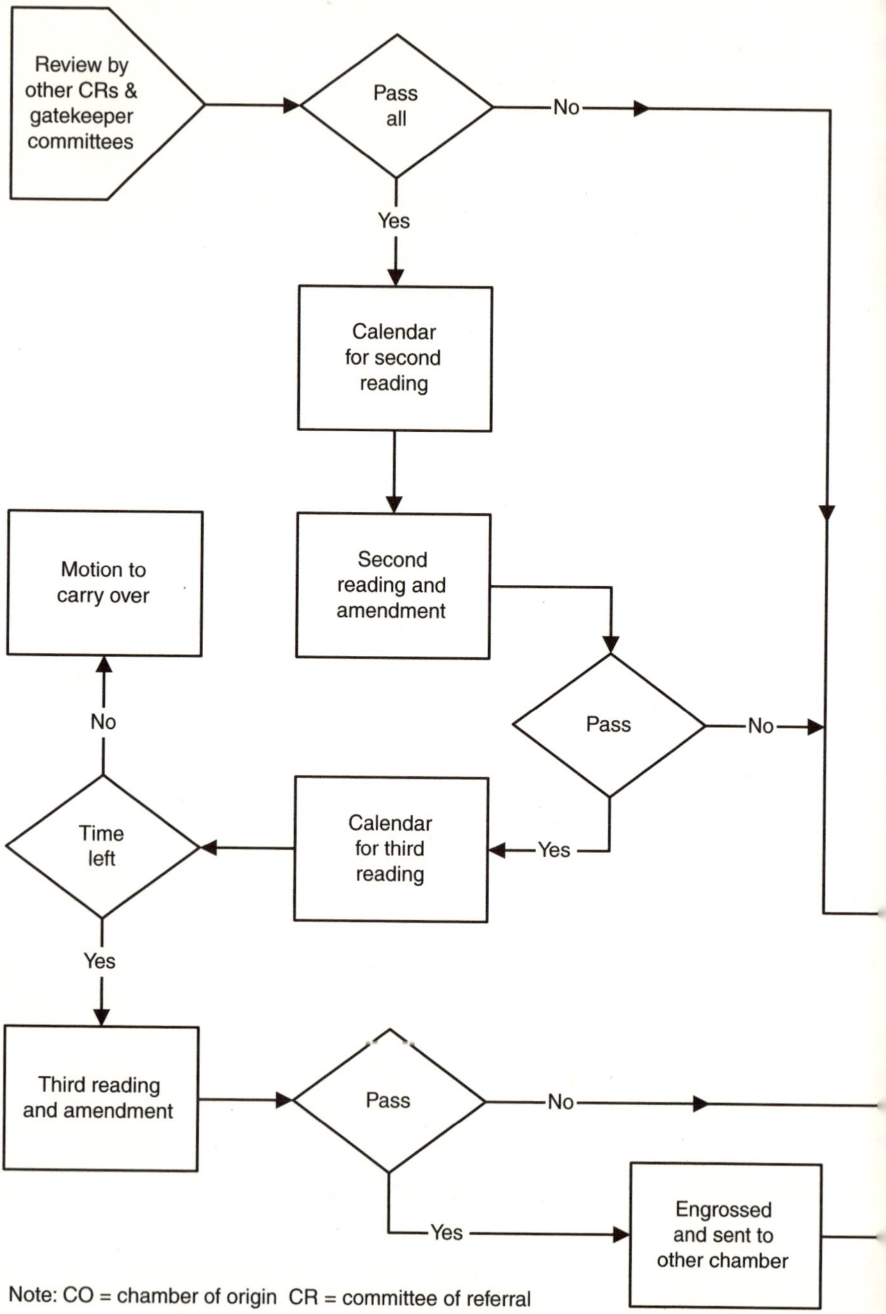

Note: CO = chamber of origin CR = committee of referral

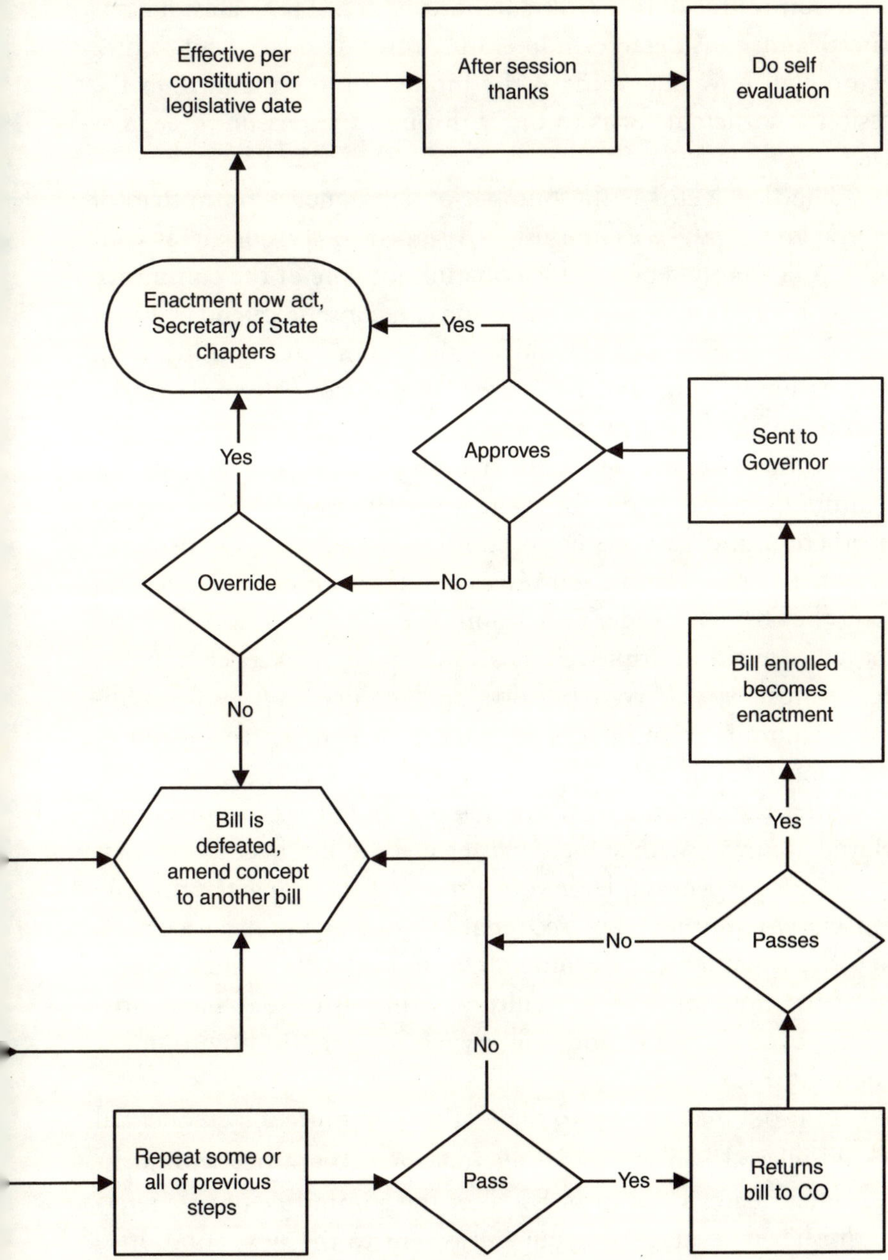

Effective per constitution or legislative date
After session thanks
Do self evaluation
Enactment now act, Secretary of State chapters
Yes
Approves
Sent to Governor
Yes
Override
No
No
Bill enrolled becomes enactment
Yes
Bill is defeated, amend concept to another bill
No
Passes
No
Repeat some or all of previous steps
Pass
Yes
Returns bill to CO

If the committee of first referral reports your bill favorably, it gains crucial and considerable momentum towards enactment. Three factors will now determine if the limited time remaining in the session is sufficient for it to move through the remaining legislative steps.

The first factor is the number of subsequent committees of referral and *gatekeeper* committees assigned to consider it. If your bill was favorably reported by a unanimous vote of the committee of first referral, it is now eligible for the consent calendar. Once placed on the calendar, it avoids further committee consideration and reading(s) and will be passed as non-controversial by the chamber within the next two weeks.

If your bill was reported favorably but is not eligible for unanimous consent, one or more committees of subject matter jurisdiction and gatekeeper committees may need to consider it further. The number of committees to review your bill will depend upon the chamber leader's intentions regarding it, how well it was drafted to avoid multiple referrals, and which gatekeeper committees it must pass. If your bill does not require a review by additional committees of referral or gatekeeper committees, it moves to second reading.

After the committee of first referral, the other committees of referral are those with subject matter jurisdiction over all or parts of your bill. For example, if your proposed bill impacts primarily impacts environment but secondarily touches upon agriculture, then the chamber's Environment committee will be the committee of first referral. The Agricultural Committee may have jurisdiction over part of it and will review it after the Environment Committee finishes.

Your bill may be sent to these other committees by sequential or split referral.[1] In sequential referral, each committee with jurisdiction evaluates it, in turn. So, after the committee of first referral finishes its evaluation, your bill is sent to the next committee of referral for evaluation of the portion of the bill within its jurisdiction. There is no limit to the number of committees of referral to which your bill may be sent and any committee of referral may amend or defeat it. If your bill receives a number of referrals, it will not have enough time in the session to pass through all of the required committees. Therefore, it will miss deadlines and be defeated.

Split referrals require committees to meet together to consider your bill. Because the agendas of all committees are very full, the likelihood of scheduling a meeting is small. Therefore, your bill may never be taken up.

The other type of committee that your bill may encounter after the committees of subject matter jurisdiction are gatekeeper committees. Gatekeeper committees are committees of referral charged with evaluating all bills for broad impacts on the state or for procedural matters. They are the money committees such as Budget and Tax which evaluates the impacts of bills upon the state budget, Government Operations which evaluates the impacts on state agencies and local governments, and Rules which assures the legality of all bills as they move to third reading.

When your bill was written, the Management Team charged the Drafting Team with writing a bill that would avoid multiple referrals as much as possible. If they were successful, your bill:

1. Was narrow in scope and reviewed only by the committee of first referral
2. Was non-controversial and eligible for unanimous consent
3. Was not reviewed by the money committees because it did not require the appropriations of state funds or enactment of new taxes
4. Was not reviewed by the Government Operations Committee because it did not affect state or local government

5. Was legal, remained unchanged throughout all readings, and was calendared for third reading by the Rules Committee

When your bill successfully passes through all committees of referral it must pass two more readings and votes in the full chamber. Then it must repeat some or all of the process in the other chamber.

If any committee reports your bill unfavorably or does not report it at all, the likelihood of enactment is greatly reduced. Speak to your sponsor about strategies to rescue it. While parliamentary options exist in theory, in practice the most likely strategy will be to amend the main points of your bill to another that is moving forward toward enactment.

A second factor affecting your bill is companion legislation. If both chambers have reported your bill favorably in the same form, it will save time by not needing to repeat the process in the other chamber. One chamber will receive the engrossed bill, move it to third reading, pass it, and return it to the chamber of origin.

The third factor affecting your bill is amendments. For as long as your bill is viable, opponents will try to amend it unfavorably or defeat it in other committees or on the floor. Your bill may also be burdened with amendments as the supporters of other bills try to use it as a vehicle to carry their stalled bills to enactment. Amendments can slow or stop your bill's passage through the enactment process.

You must continue to build momentum for your issue by lobbying for your bill at every opportunity. Lobby every committee through which your bill must pass by speaking to the chair to gain a sense of how the committee will look upon it. If he or she indicates that your bill may not pass the committee or may be amended unfavorably, you will also need to lobby the committee's members.

You must be present at every committee meeting or chamber session that considers your bill to help your sponsor protect it from stalling, shield it from burdensome amendments, and prevent unfavorable votes. Once your bill passes both chambers in the same form, it will be enrolled (certified) and sent to the Governor for signature. If it does not pass in identical form, one chamber or the other will need to amend its bill to make it identical or adopt the other chamber's version. If this does not occur, your bill is defeated.

You may need to lobby the Governor to gain his or her favorable treatment of your bill. Despite successful passage of all the required steps, including being sent to the Governor for a final signature, he or she can either permit it to become law or veto it. In some cases, the Governor may demand changes to the bill in order to avoid a veto.

As the session is expiring, investigate your state's carry over provisions, if any. In some states, bills that were not passed but were not defeated are automatically carried over to be re-introduced next year. However, in others states, the sponsor must ask the chamber to grant carry over privileges for the bill. In states without carry over, the bill must be reintroduced next year.

After the session

If you were successful and your bill was enacted into law, congratulations! However, if it was not enacted then you should capitalize on the legislative momentum that you built this year to carry your bill farther next year.

If your bill passed, thank those legislators who supported it. If the new law will accomplish a genuine public good, write letters-to-the-editor or purchase advertisements in district newspapers praising the bill and the legislators' contributions. You may also send a press release to the media that explains the good of the bill and a legislator's role in its enactment. Ask important persons, organizations, and companies to send letters of thanks to those lawmakers who helped. Praise key legislators in as many forums as possible, including organization newsletters.

If your bill became law with the Governor's signature, consider asking him or her for a *signing ceremony.* If the Governor has an opening in his or her schedule and can benefit politically, he or she may participate in a ceremony that re-enacts the signing of your bill into law. Here, you can gather mementos, such as photographs with the Governor, copies of the signed bill and pens bearing the Governor's name. Be aware that your bill will likely become law before the ceremony can take place. If your bill became a law without the Governor's signature, then do not ask for a re-enactment of something that never took place.

Hold an awards ceremony to honor your main sponsor and present him or her with a plaque. Call the award the "Legislator of the Year" or something similar and present it at a state-wide meeting.

Encourage your association members to remember the re-election campaigns of supportive legislators with financial and other contributions. Ask them to invite those legislators to visit their organizations or to attend social events. Invite lawmakers to visit employees or at least visit the facility to greet them going to, leaving, or at work.

Thank any staff persons who were especially helpful and emphasize their contribution to their legislator or superior. This includes committee, personal staff, and secretaries. Inform helpful associations of your appreciation for their support. Consider giving your contract lobbyist a bonus.

If your bill did not pass, send a short note of thanks to lawmakers, associations, and others that interacted with you. Tell your supporters that you will be back again next year and that you hope they will support you. To those lawmakers who did not support your bill, politely and briefly restate your case for adoption and state that you hope to satisfy their concerns next year.

Remember that failure to see enactment in a session does not mean that you have failed. You have been successful if you generated momentum and interest in your bill. Depending upon jurisdiction, as much as 50% to 90% of bills do not pass the first time. A bill often takes three or more years of lobbying before it becomes law. Your efforts in the first year likely built a foundation of relationships and momentum that will move you forward in the next year or later sessions.

Whether your bill passed or not, thank the members of your association who participated in the lobbying effort. Recognize the accomplishments of the key person(s) in your association who worked on behalf of the bill. If they served at their employers' directions, compliment them in a thank you note written to the employers.

Next, complete the internal and external evaluations. Look critically at the main sponsor and co-sponsors, consultants including the contract lobbyists, and all persons inside and outside of your association who worked on the bill. Consider:

1. If your bill did not become law, do you still need the legislative relief that the bill would have brought?
2. If you formed an *ad hoc* association, should you keep it for another year or form a new one? If you are a permanent association, are you the best group to lobby or should you form a new association?
3. Should an entirely different group lobby this issue next year?
4. How did your association interact with your members, member companies, or member organizations? Did you coordinate efforts well or did their legislative activities conflict with yours?
5. What will your internal association politics be next year?

6. Was your communication effective?
7. How well did you work with your supporters? Did each of you follow through on commitments to each other? Would you want an alliance with them again next year?
8. How well did you work with your opponents? Could you have blunted their opposition better in some way?
9. Could you develop a bill that you and your opponents might be able to support next session?
10. Did you make any new enemies? If you did, what is their significance? Did you amend your concepts onto someone else's bill and cause it to stall or be defeated?
11. Evaluate your consultant(s) including your contract lobbyist. How well did each meet your expectations? How did lawmakers and staff respond to the contract lobbyist(s)? Did you work well with him or her? Should you renew or not renew the contract? What changes are needed for next year?
12. Was your sponsor effective? Do you want to work with the same sponsor next year or should another legislator be approached for sponsorship? Would your sponsor want to sponsor the bill again? Would he or she release "ownership" of the bill to another lawmaker?
13. Which lawmakers surprised you as supporters or as opponents?
14. How did the Governor or executive offices impact your effort? Can you obtain their support in the future?
15. What will the capitol politics be next year?
16. How effective were your negotiations?
17. Evaluate your own performance. Who among you was effective? Who might be better suited for a new assignment next year?
18. What additional help could you have used?
19. What would you have done differently? Does any one event stand out as the turning point in the success or failure of your

bill? How did you respond to this event and how should you have responded?

20. Will there be enough member consensus and commitment to try again next year?

Summary

If you are in the first of a two-year legislative session and your bill is still alive, you may have the advantage of carry over. Estimate the likelihood of moving your bill in the second year and begin lobbying immediately after lawmakers have had time to rest after the first year.

If this was the second year of a two-year session and your bill did not pass, wait to see how the intervening elections will affect the Governor and legislature's membership. If there is a great shift in political power in the capitol, you may need to start from the beginning. However, because of the experience gained and relationships established, you will start from a stronger position.

After completing the evaluation exercise ask yourself again, "Is a bill still necessary?" If the answer is "Yes," ask "Do we want to try again?" If the answer to this second question is "Yes," then go to the beginning of this book and start the process again. This time, however, you will be experienced lobbyist(s) who will know how to lobby your bill into law.

---

1 Sequential and split referrals are dangerous for your bill. If the leader of the chamber wants to defeat it quietly, he or she may give it multiple or split referrals.

Engineering THE LAW, Inc.

The Art and Science of Legislation

Engineering THE LAW, Incorporated trains new state lobbyists and assists groups with their state lobbying efforts. This user-friendly reference has been developed with the new lobbyist in mind. Its goal is to guide the efforts of those who seek to use the American state legislative system to find solutions for existing, recurrent, or emerging issues.

In addition to this book, ETL offers a one day comprehensive seminar about lobbying. Details about the seminar may be found on the Internet at http://www.learn-to-lobby.com. Additional information about the services provided by ETL or the seminar may be obtained by contacting Mr. Robert Guyer at

P.O. Box 35-7425,
Gainesville, FL 32635-7425
rlguyer@learn-to-lobby.com

Robert L. Guyer serves as President of ETL. Previously, Mr. Guyer served as Legislative Counsel and Assistant Director, State Government Affairs for Ralston Purina Company. He worked with Energizer Power Systems, a division of Eveready Battery Company, Inc., and with Gates Energy Products, Inc. in legislative affairs. Other legislative experience has been gained in the electric utility industry, a regulatory agency, and consulting. As a team player with numerous industry associations, he has successfully helped lobby laws to enactment in several states and in Washington, D.C. Mr. Guyer holds degrees in law, civil engineering, and political science and is admitted to the practice of law in the State of Florida and the District of Columbia.

Laura K. Guyer, Ph.D. serves as Vice-President of ETL. Dr. Guyer was previously a tenured Associate Professor and Director of Dietetics Programs at the University of Florida in Gainesville. She has worked as a consultant and clinician in adult medicine, long term care, and wellness in several health care organizations. As a member of the Administrative Council of the Florida Dietetic Association, Dr. Guyer worked with others to develop an effective lobbying campaign. Dr. Guyer holds degrees in Food Science and Human Nutrition, Adult Education, and Curriculum and Instruction. You may contact Dr. Guyer at

P.O. Box 35-7425,
Gainesville, FL 32635-7425
lkguyer@learn-to-lobby.com

Glossary

Each state uses its own legislative terminology. However, some terms have the same meaning in all states, some have different meanings in different states and some are unique to a particular state. This glossary is a compilation of terms extracted from lobbying experience and several state-published glossaries. It is designed to provide an overview of legislative terms that you may encounter as you lobby. Be sure, however, to obtain a state-specific glossary of terms prior to lobbying in a particular legislature.

Act An enactment that has become law.

- *Private Act or Local Act* Applies to a person or limited area or subdivision of government.
- *Public Act* Applies to the entire state or is of a general nature with local application.

Action How the legislature handles or responds to a measure placed before it, including any steps of parliamentary procedure taken.

Acts of the Senate, House, or Assembly The bound annual compilation of all legislation passed by the body that became law, and certain resolves and resolutions.

Adjournment Termination of a session or meeting for that day with the hour and day of the next meeting being set prior to adjournment. It is also cessation of the legislative session for the year or biennium. See also *Sine Die.*

Adoption In general, the passage by a committee, chamber, or legislature of measures, bills, memorials, amendments, resolves, or resolutions. In procedural parlance, the term is often limited to describing the acceptance of amendments or resolutions.

Advance Sheets Bound copies of laws and resolutions enacted during a legislative session prior to incorporation into the codified laws of the state. Individual copies of laws prior to binding are called *slip laws.*

Amend To change a bill, motion, report, or another amendment by adding, deleting, or changing language. Only the chamber can amend a measure. In almost all states, committee amendments are, in fact, committee recommendations that the chamber adopt the proposed changes. While committee amendments are technically suggestions, in fact, ninety-five percent of committee recommendations are followed. Thus, while technically incorrect, for practical purposes a committee can be said to "amend" legislation.

Amendment Formal wording, either spoken or written, changing or proposing to change the language of a bill or measure. Amendments are made on a line-by-line, word-by-word basis and are voted upon individually. There are many types of amendments, including:

- *Author's, Sponsor's, or Patron's Amendment* Proposed by the bill's main sponsor anytime after bill introduction.
- *Floor Amendment* Proposed to the chamber by the amendment sponsor.
- *Hostile Amendment* Opposed by the main sponsor of the bill.
- *Amendment in the Nature of a Substitute* An amendment so extensive that it constitutes a new bill.

Appropriation The amount of money set aside or earmarked for a particular purpose by a bill. Often, this is the money necessary to implement the bill should it become law.

Approved by the Governor Signature of the Governor on an enrolled bill. Sometimes a bill is stamped "Approved by the Governor" to indicate executive approval.

Archives, Legislative Public records, including copies of all measures considered at each session, journals, committee reports, and other documents usually kept by the Secretary of State, Legislative Librarian, or other state document officer.

Author, Sponsor or Patron Person(s) or committee(s) listed on the bill as responsible for it in the chamber of origin. Sometimes *chief author, main sponsor, lead sponsor,* or a similar term is used to indicate the primary individual(s). Some states limit the number of sponsors or co-sponsors on a bill or the total number of bills a lawmaker may sponsor in a session.

- *Co-sponsor* A secondary sponsor with lesser responsibility for a bill.
- *Joint sponsor* One of two or more sponsors with equal responsibility for a bill.

Bicameral A legislative body composed of two chambers; the Senate or Upper Chamber and the House, Assembly, or Lower Chamber. Except for Nebraska, which has a unicameral or one-chamber legislature, all U.S. state legislatures are bicameral.

Biennium A two-year term of legislative activity.

Bill A proposal to create, change, or repeal a law.

- *Amendatory Bills* Propose section-by-section modifications of existing law.
- *Independent Bills* Propose a new law.
- *Repealing Bills* Propose to revoke a law.

Bill Analysis A written analysis of a bill prepared by a legislative services agency or a committee of referral explaining the bill and expected impacts on the state. It contains background information and fiscal and other impacts.

Bill, Anatomy of Includes the caption, chamber coding, the title, the enacting clause, the body of language to be enacted, the effective date, and summary.

- *Body* The language that will become law. The proposed wording must be identified, clearly indicating added and deleted words.
- *Caption* A brief description of a bill's contents appearing on the first page.
- *Chamber coding* Informs the reader of the chamber of origin, reference number, sponsor(s) and date of introduction. It may also convey limited information as to status, such as whether the bill is a substitute, which in a series of substitutes, and whether it has been engrossed or enrolled. Coding includes the method of clearly identifying new, added, deleted, or repealed language.
- *Effective date* Establishes the date the law takes effect. Sections of the bill or provisions in the bill may take effect at times other than the date the bill itself takes effect.
- *Enacting clause* Conveys the intent of the legislature that the bill, if enacted, would be a state law. The wording of the enacting clause is found in the state constitution. Generally, all language after the enacting clause is law and everything above it is not.
- *Summary* Explains the bill in a few sentences. It is found on the first or last page of the bill.
- *Title* Conveys the subject matter of the bill. An amendatory or repealing bill additionally states the sections of existing law

affected. State constitutions and chamber practice require that a bill specifically state which sections are being amended, deleted, or repealed and show the entire section with changes in context clearly identified.

Bill Back, Bill Cover, or Bill Envelope The protective cover for a bill, resolution, or other measure displaying the bill number and title, often with lines for signatures of sponsors and co-sponsors. They may be color coded for each chamber and type of measure, such as blue for a House bill, green for a House resolution, pink for a Senate bill, goldenrod for a Senate resolution, orange for a joint resolution, etc.

Bill Draft Request or Legislative Request A lawmaker's request which initiates the drafting of a bill by Legislative Counsel or other bill drafting services. The number associated with the request may identify the bill for the session.

Bill Folder The file or similar folder containing the original bill, proposed amendments, committee report, memoranda, records of votes, and other historical information surrounding the life of a particular bill during the legislative session.

Bill Room, Legislative Document Room, or Bill Distribution Room The room from which a legislative agency distributes all printed bills, measures, calendars, and digests. The *enrolling room* is the room where bills are engrossed, re-engrossed, or enrolled and may be proximate to or part of the bill room.

Bills, Types of Independent and amendatory bills can be categorized in a number of ways based upon procedure or substance. A few of the varieties or designations of bills include the following:

- *Amended Bill* A bill as changed by amendments.
- *Appropriations* or *Budget Bill* Proposes the state budget or individual appropriations.
- *Bond Bill* Authorizes the sale of a state's general obligation bonds to finance specified projects or activities.
- *Charter Bill* Relates to powers of local government.
- *Committee Bill* Sponsored by a committee.
- *Companion Bills* Identical bills introduced in each chamber, often simultaneously.
- *Conference Bill* Sent to a conference committee or reported by a conference committee to the chambers.
- *Deficiency Bill* or *Supplemental Appropriations Bill* A bill appropriating additional monies for items in which the original appropriation was inadequate.
- *District, Local, Local Uncontested,* or *Private Bill* Affects only a particular district or small geographical area, normally enacted at the request of the legislators representing the affected district; also, a bill affecting only one person.
- *Draft Bill* A bill that is given to the legislative services agency to be drafted for introduction; also, a bill given to the Clerk or Secretary prior to first printing, after which it becomes an original bill.
- *Emergency Bill* Deals with some immediate problem. It becomes effective upon super majority vote and Governor's signature or shortly thereafter rather than on the date prescribed by the constitution. See also *Emergency Clause.*
- *Engrossed Bill* A bill corrected to include all amendments passed by a chamber.
- *Enrolled Bill* Passed by both chambers and certified by the Speaker and President.
- *Errors, "Glitch,"* or *Conforming Bill* These correct non-substantive technical errors in earlier enacted legislation.

- *Fiscal Bill* A measure appropriating funds or requiring a state agency to spend money for a specified purpose.
- *Governor's Bill* Advocated by the Governor. Some states exempt Governor's bills from certain legislative procedures.
- *Money* or *Tax Bill* Proposes taxes.
- *Omnibus* or *Train Bill* A large bill covering a multitude of matters related to a single subject.
- *Original Bill* A bill as first filed with the chamber Clerk or Secretary.
- *Pre-filed Bill* An original bill filed before the start of the legislative session.
- *Proposed Committee Bill* Proposed by a committee, but not yet introduced.
- *Proposed Bill* Prior to introduction and during pre-session, these bills are printed by the chamber, distributed to the public, and studied by committees. The resulting original bill is able to move much more quickly through the legislature.
- *Public* or *General Bill* Affects the entire state or several areas of a state.
- *Reported Bill* Reported by a committee to the chamber.
- *Resolution Bill* See Resolution.
- *Spot, Skeleton,* or *Vehicle Bill* A bill with little substance intended to be amended later with the addition of substantive text. The added text must be of the same subject area as the spot bill.
- *Stand-alone* or *Free-standing Bill* Dedicated to one matter alone as distinguished from a bill carrying many concepts.
- *Study Bill* Proposes that a study be undertaken prior to taking further legislative action.
- *Substitute Bill* Offered in place of the original bill.

Budget The Governor's annual or biannual requested allocation of state monies to operate state government.

By Request A bill introduced by a legislator at the request of a constituent or other party. *By request* may indicate that the legislator has little interest in the fate of the bill.

Calendar, Agenda, or File The listing of bills eligible for debate; the daily printed agenda of business for each chamber often containing scheduled committee meetings and public hearings. Types of calendars include, but are not limited to:

- *Consent Calendar* Lists bills awaiting a vote for unanimous consent.
- *Final Calendar* or *Resume* The compilation of legislative calendars for a session.
- *Legislative Calendar* A chronological status summary of all actions taken on all bills.
- *Special Orders Calendar* Lists bills awaiting second reading.
- *Regular Calendar* Lists the bills awaiting third reading.

Call of the House or Senate On motion by a chamber member, the presiding officer directs the Sergeant-at-Arms to lock the chamber and bring in the absent members, by arrest if necessary, to vote on a measure under consideration. No action is taken on an item under call until the call is lifted, at which time it must be voted upon immediately. Members may not pass or otherwise refuse to vote when a vote comes as a result of a call of the chamber.

Call to Order The presiding officer's proclamation that the chamber or committee is officially beginning its session.

Capital The city in which the seat of state government is located. The Governor, legislature, and other state officers are located in the capital. See *Political Capital.*

Capitol The building, normally grand and imposing, in which the legislature has its main meeting chambers, one large room for the Senate and one larger room for the House. Other meeting rooms and governmental offices, including those of the Governor and state officers, may be located there as well.

Carry or Carrying a Bill To sponsor or work for enactment of a bill. Only legislators can "carry" a bill.

Carry Over To continue a bill that is introduced during the first year of a two-year session to the second year if it does not complete the legislative process by the end of the first year. The bill retains its bill number and is automatically reintroduced at the beginning of the second year. In states without automatic carry over, unenacted bills are defeated at the end of the annual term, except by special action of the legislature.

Casting or Tie-Breaking Vote The deciding vote cast by the Lieutenant Governor or President when there is a tie vote in the Senate or by the Speaker in the House.

Caucus As a noun, a group of legislators who form an interest bloc in the chamber because of their common interest in a specific issue or topic. As a verb, the coming together of the group for discussion. A "binding caucus," illegal in some states, is one in which all members are bound to support the decision of the caucus.

Chair, Chairman, Chairwoman, or Chairperson The legislator appointed to preside over an individual committee or subcommittee.

Chamber(s) The building containing the large rooms in which the legislature meets; also called a *hall.* It is the room designated for the formal assembly of legislators to conduct the business of one chamber, i.e. the Senate or House, of the legislature. It is also another name for the Senate or House in its official capacity.

Clerk of the House or Assembly A non-legislator normally elected by the members to serve as the chief administrator of the House.

Chapter or Chaptered An act becomes effective when the public is given notice of its requirements through publication by the Secretary of State. An act assigned a *chapter number* and published in the session laws is *chaptered* and becomes law. On the effective date, its provisions are legally binding.

Chapter Out The nullification of one or more portions of an earlier passed bill that has provisions that conflict with provisions of one passed later. The bill last in time is first in authority.

Citator See *Daily File.*

Co-Author, Co-Sponsor, or Co-Patron A legislator whose name appears after the main sponsor's on a bill. An *original* co-sponsor adds his or her name to the bill before it is introduced into the chamber.

Codes Bound volumes of state statutory law organized by subject matter.

Comment, Public or Citizen Statements about a bill issued by non-committee members during the time allocated for comments in the public hearing portion of a committee meeting. It is less formal than *formal testimony* on a bill. See *Testimony, Formal.*

Committee A distinct subgroup of legislators charged with considering all bills related to a certain area of subject matter. Most state legislatures have numerous committees appointed by the leadership of a chamber, a few of which include the following categories:

- *Ad hoc Committee* A temporary committee established to accomplish a specific and limited task. Upon completion, the committee is dissolved.
- *Conference Committee* A temporary committee appointed to work toward reconciling differences between chambers over a single bill. When its task is finished, the committee is disbanded. In some states, the conference committee is limited to considering only those matters in dispute. In others, the committee may consider any portion of the bill. A *free conference committee* is authorized to consider any portion of a bill, including the addition of entirely new provisions.
- *Gatekeeper Committee* Standing committee charged with evaluating most or all bills for impact upon budget, taxes, legality, effects on local government, state agencies, and similar non-subject matter concerns. The committee evaluates and may certify, for example, that a bill has no impact on local government, does or does not impose requirements on state government operations, or is legally correct. It may amend a bill within its narrow area of authority.
- *Interim* or *Study Committee* A committee, often joint, charged with studying and reporting back to the chamber or legislature on a particular topic. It meets during the interim between legislative sessions and may include non-legislators. It may be called *ad hoc, select,* or *task force.*
- *Joint Committee* Consist of members from each chamber and is established cooperatively by both. In certain states, it is the primary working committee.
- *Money Committee* Charged with handling appropriations,

variously called Appropriations, Budget, Finance, Finance and Tax, or Ways and Means.

- *Oversight Committee* Charged with ongoing review of one or more parts of the *executive branch.*
- *Select, Special,* or *Study Committee* Established by the presiding officer to report to him or her and then to the chamber; or a committee authorized to study a certain topic.
- *Standing Committee* A more or less permanent committee established by a chamber or jointly by the chambers to focus on a particular area of legislation such as agriculture, welfare, business, etc., or as gatekeepers.
- *Statutory Committee* A more or less permanent committee established by law and, as such, less subject to the will of the leadership of a single chamber.

Committee of Referral A committee which has jurisdiction over a bill in whole or in part and through which a bill must pass in order to proceed to the next step. The *committee of first referral* is the committee with jurisdiction over the main subject matter of a bill and is the first substantive committee to consider a bill in detail.

Committee of the Whole The entire chamber meeting as a committee to consider bills, most often prior to second reading. It usually operates with a smaller quorum than is required for the entire chamber, uses relaxed rules of debate, and is chaired by the Speaker, President, or a legislator appointed by one of them.

Concur or Concurrence The chamber of origin approves or adopts a bill amended by the other chamber. In *non-concurrence,* the chamber of origin rejects the amended bill and it is sent to a conference committee or is defeated.

Conferees Officially designated members of a conference committee.

Conflict Bill language that, usually unintentionally, contradicts another existing amendment, bill, or statutory or constitutional law with the same purpose.

Conflict of Interest The conflict between a representative's unique personal interest in the outcome of an act and the good of those he or she is representing. Conflict of interest threatens the ability of representatives to faithfully carry out their duties.

Consent Calendar A listing of non-controversial bills that skip second and third readings and move to the floor for a unanimous vote of the chamber. By virtue of being favorably reported by unanimous vote of committee(s) of referral, bills are placed on the consent calendar. Members are polled in advance of the vote to ensure unanimous support of the bill.

Constituent A person who lives or works in a legislator's electoral district.

Constitution The written fundamental legal principles of a state which can be changed, not by the legislature, but by the majority vote of the people.

Convene Members of the legislature gathering together to engage in official legislative business.

Daily File, List, Book, File, Citator, Schedule, or Agenda A list of chamber activities for a given day. It includes bills to be considered at forthcoming committee meetings, bills in conference, bills eligible for consideration during the next scheduled floor session (whether on special order or for *second* or *third reading),* committee assignments, the current legislative calendar, and bills which are ready but will not be considered that day (sometimes called the *inactive file).* Some legislatures combine their daily files into a joint legislative schedule that covers both chambers.

Debate Formal argumentation according to the rules of the chamber.

Desk The location of the Clerk, Secretary, or clerical staffs on the chamber floor. The desk is located in front of or next to the rostrum of the presiding officer. It also refers to the staff and offices of the Secretary or Clerk. The *member's desk* is the desk assigned to a member on the floor. A member may vote only from his or her desk. The term *to place on the desk or put across the desk* refers to the act of introducing a bill or resolution by presenting it, with the necessary accompanying paperwork, to the Clerk or Secretary. *The desk is clear* means that there is no further business before the chamber.

Digest, Legislative Counsel's Digest, Measure Summary, or Summary Written by a legislative services agency, this is a brief impartial summary of the changes, additions or deletions that a bill proposes to make to existing law. The digest accompanies a bill and may be found on its first or last page. The digest may also refer to a listing of all bills with the summary and final action considered during a session. It is sometimes called *bulletin of proceedings* or *final history.*

Digester A *legislative services agency* that prepares brief summaries of proposed legislation.

District The geographical area encompassing the citizens represented by a legislator.

Docket A list of bills pending before a committee.

Effective Date The date on which an act becomes law, that is, binding. The state constitution establishes the effective date. However, by super majority vote, the legislature may set an earlier effective date for a particular bill. Provisions within a bill may have later effective dates than does the bill, itself.

Emergency Clause The provision in an emergency bill that moves the effective date forward, often to the day the enactment bill is signed by the Governor.

Enabling Legislation Requires or authorizes an executive agency to take certain actions, including the adoption of administrative rules, to implement a public law.

Enacting Clause The constitutionally required phrase on a bill that formally expresses the legislature's intent that a bill become law. It is generally in the form, "Be it enacted by the Legislature of the State of ____."

Enactment Final passage of a bill by both chambers and enrollment, followed by the Governor allowing the bill to become law by signing it or failing to veto it within a constitutionally established period of time. If the Governor vetoes the bill, it may be enacted by a super majority vote of both chambers.

Engross The incorporation of adopted amendments into the text of a bill. A bill is engrossed after second and third readings and upon return from the other chamber. The bill is reprinted each time it is engrossed.

- *Official engrossment* The chamber of origin passes a bill as amended by the other chamber.

- *Unofficial engrossment* The amendment and passage of a bill by the chamber not originating the bill.

Enroll or Ratify The leaders of both chambers, by their signatures, certify that the bill has been passed by the two chambers and is an enactment.

Executive The Governor.

Executive Agency An administrative department reporting to the Governor that assists him or her in carrying out the Governor's duties. These agencies include the departments of Environmental Protection, Business Regulation, Health, and similar offices.

Executive Order A document signed by the Governor that establishes policy for the executive agencies, but which has no statutory or administrative legal standing.

Executive Session A private, official meeting of legislators from which others are excluded. Executive sessions usually consider highly sensitive issues. No formal actions that affect a bill occur during an executive session.

Ex Officio The holding of an office by virtue of holding another, usually high, office. *Ex officio* offices are usually non-voting members of committees. The chamber leader is an *ex officio* member of all committees.

File Number In some states, this is a bill's identification number while in others, it is the number of a bill in the daily file.

Fiscal Statement or Note, Economic Impact Statement A statement of estimated future costs and benefits to the state should a bill become law.

Floor This is the portion of the large meeting room in which the entire chamber routinely meets that is reserved for legislators to conduct official business. It is separated from the *gallery*. The term also indicates that the entire membership is considering a bill. The phrase "on the floor" indicates that a bill is being debated by the chamber. The debate sessions are floor periods or floor sessions. The term also signifies that the legislature is in formal daily session.

Floor Leader A leadership position in a chamber, one for the majority and one for the minority. The *majority floor leader* is second to the Speaker or President. The floor leader is second to the President pro tempore in states in which the Lieutenant Governor is the President. The *minority floor leader* is the minority party's chief policy and political strategist and is its highest position in the chamber. Less frequently, the term refers to a legislator chosen by the Governor to represent his or her views and to serve as a liaison between the Governor and the chamber.

Floor Manager The legislator responsible for shepherding a bill on the floor. This is usually the main sponsor. However, if the main sponsor is not a member of the *committee of first referral,* the chair may appoint a member from the committee to advance the bill.

Gallery Balconies in the chamber from which visitors view proceedings of the chamber.

Germane Relevant to the subject matter of a bill, topic, or discussion.

Grandfather To exempt current activities from the requirements of a new law.

Hearing, Public A meeting of a committee or subcommittee to consider a specific bill in which public comment, formal testimony, or both, is received.

History Sheet A paper that covers the original bill folder and summarizes the key steps and dates in the progress of an original bill.

Hopper The name given to the bill clerk's in-box which contains bills awaiting introduction.

House or Assembly One of two bodies of a bicameral legislature, the other being the Senate. The House has the greater number of members, they are elected by smaller districts, and they usually serve for shorter terms than Senators.

Initiative A proposed law placed on the ballot by petition of a constitutionally established percentage of voters.

Interim The time interval between sessions. Committees often study subject matters for future bills during the interim.

Introduce or Introduction In accord with established chamber procedures, the formal presentation of a bill and its accompanying information to the Bill Clerk for consideration by the chamber.

Journal or Journals of the Chamber The minutes or official chronological record of the proceedings of a chamber. The *daily journal* is the daily legislative record of the chamber's floor and committee activities and messages from the Governor. "Let the record show" or "let the record reflect" is a request that the journal contain the item that is the subject of the request. The *session journal* is a compendium of daily journals that have been certified by the appropriate officer, indexed, and bound.

Jurisdiction The subject matter over which a legislative body has authority called subject matter jurisdiction. The geographical area in which a law applies.

Law Formal rules governing certain aspects of human interaction, as enacted by the legislature or by the people, or as authorized by the legislature to be decreed by an executive agency.

- *Advance Sheet* A compilation of state laws before codification into statutes.
- *Private Law* or *Special Law* Has limited applicability and is not codified.
- *Public Law* A law of general applicability, codified as *statutory laws.*
- *Resolve Law* A type of private law of temporary duration.
- *Session Law, Law of the State,* or *Compiled Law* All private, special, and public laws, constitutional resolutions, resolves, and joint resolutions enacted during the legislative session.
- *Slip Law* An individual printed law enacted by the legislature that has not yet been codified.

Legislative Analyst A legislative services agency staff person charged with providing non-partisan analyses of proposed legislation.

Legislative Council or Legislative Coordinating Council A formal or informal committee of the leadership of both chambers, often minority and majority parties, which meet to coordinate and manage the activities of the separate chambers. Between sessions, it meets to oversee interim committees and represent the legislature.

Legislative Counsel An appointed or elected non-partisan officer charged with ensuring that bills are correct with regard to law and form. He or she also represents the legislature in legal matters.

Legislative History The compilation of available information regarding the enactment of a bill. It includes the original file folder, specific memoranda, tapes, or transcripts of committee meetings, minutes, and other information. Especially in judicial and administrative proceedings, the history is often used to determine *legislative intent.* It and other materials are often stored in the state's legislative library or archives.

Legislative Intent The legislature's identification of what it wants the bill to accomplish. It includes information about the problem to be fixed, the reasoning that supports its enactment, and the bill's purpose. The preamble, the bill itself, the billfolder including minutes, tapes, history, and other records can be used to determine legislative intent.

Legislative Liaison The contact person from an executive agency or Governor's office to the legislature.

Legislative Manual A guide to the legislature, published each biennium by a chamber or legislature, that contains information about the members, staff, room locations, and the chamber and its processes.

Legislative Procedure or Process The series of several steps that all bills follow through the legislature as they proceed to become laws. The legislative process begins with introduction and continues until the bill becomes law or is defeated.

Legislative Services Agencies Offices created by the legislature to assist with drafting bills, resolutions, amendments and digests, and to provide opinions on facts and law. These offices have different names such as: Legislative Counsel, Legislative Services Office, Legislative Bureau, Bill Drafting Service, Legislative

Research Department, Reviser of Statutes, Legislative Administrative Services, and others.

Legislator A representative elected by the people in an electoral district sent to participate in the lawmaking branch of state government known as the legislature.

Legislature The branch of government charged with legislating, that is, creating laws. *Citizen legislatures* or *part-time legislatures* meet for a short time each year or biennium. *Professional* or *full-time* legislatures meet year round. It is also a two-year legislative session. If used to describe a time period, the word is preceded by a number indicating which two-year session is being described, as in the "73rd Legislature."

Lieutenant Governor Second to the Governor in the executive branch. In a number of states, the Lieutenant Governor is also the President of the Senate. In a few states, he or she wields considerable power over legislative matters, including appointing committees and their chairs, referring legislation to committees, controlling floor debate, and recognizing Senators wishing to speak.

Lobbyist, Legislative Advocate, or Legislative Agent A person who tries to influence legislation on behalf of others. States require formal registration as a lobbyist upon triggering statutory requirements. Registration and reporting requirements vary widely among the states.

Majority Party The political party that has more members in a chamber than the other.

Manuals of Legislative Procedure Manuals of parliamentary procedure used to direct a chamber's deliberations. *Mason's Manual of Legislative Procedure* is used in most states. *Jefferson's Manual of*

Parliamentary Procedure is used in the U.S. Congress and in a few states. *Reed's Parliamentary Rules* and *Robert's Rules of Order* are also used.

Measure or Instrument A bill, resolve, memorial, resolution, joint resolution, concurrent resolution, or constitutional amendment set before a legislature.

Message As a noun, a notice from the Governor to the legislature, legislature to Governor, or a communication between the two chambers. Messages may be printed in the journal. As a verb, the act of sending a bill to the other chamber or to the Governor, or the sending of an engrossed bill to the other chamber.

Meeting An official gathering of a committee, in person or by electronic media, for the purpose of discussing matters within the jurisdiction of the committee. See *Quorum.*

Minority Party The political party that has fewer members than the other in the chamber.

Minutes A written summary of the proceedings of a chamber or committee. A *minute book,* sometimes called a *mini-journal,* is a condensed daily record of floor actions and committee reports.

Morning Hour The time when matters not on the calendar may be considered, such as the introduction of guests or a member's discussion of any subject.

Motion A formal request for action made by a legislator during a committee hearing or floor session. A large number of motions are possible. Some motions are debatable and some are not. The following are some of the motions you may hear a lawmaker make:

- *Adhere* When the positions of the two chambers conflict over a bill, this motion asks the chamber of origin to hold to its conflicting position but does not request a conference committee. Unless the other body *recedes,* the bill is defeated.

- *Adjourn* A non-debatable motion to end the day's session.
- *Adopt a Committee Report* A non-debatable motion for the chamber to adopt a committee's report.
- *Amend* A motion to add or strike words to a bill being considered.
- *Bring Up a Bill Without Reference to File* Asks for consideration of a bill not on the daily file.
- *Change the Calendar* A motion that requests a change in the order of business listed on the daily calendar to allow an item to be taken out of the published order.
- *Close* or *Limit Debate* Proposes to end debate on a pending question immediately or at the expiration of a specified time. It does not limit debate on additional motions or amendments, nor does it call for an immediate vote on the question.
- *Commit* or *Recommit* Asks for the return of a reported bill back to the reporting committee or to a new committee for reconsideration.
- *Conform* A companion bill is made to conform to the engrossed version received from the other chamber.
- *Consider the Main Question* A motion to end debate and take a vote to pass or defeat a bill.
- *Consider the Previous Question* A motion to end debate that prevents the offering of more amendments and motions and brings approval of the pending question to an immediate vote.
- *Continue* or *Carry Over* For states without automatic carry over, this motion asks that a bill be considered in the second year of a two-year legislative session without needing to be reintroduced.
- *Correct Journal* Asks to correct any day's journal.

- *Discharge, Recall, Re-refer,* or *Withdraw* Asks the chamber to take a bill away from a committee and refer it to another committee or to the floor for action. A motion to discharge is noticed one or more days ahead of the motion by the filing of a *discharge petition.*
- *Division* A motion to vote and count each individual member through the raising of hands, standing in a line, or forcing each member to be viewed and counted by the presiding officer. Electronic voting has greatly simplified division voting.
- *Division of a Question* Asks that a matter before a body be split up into two or more separate questions, each requiring its own vote.
- *Expunge* Proposes to delete an item from the official record.
- *Insist* When the positions of the two chambers over a certain bill conflict, a motion to insist asks the chamber to stand by its previous position and request a conference committee.
- *Lay on the Table* A non-debatable motion to no longer consider the bill under discussion.
- *Pass by Indefinitely, Pass for the Day,* or *Temporarily Pass* Proposes to pass over a bill until it can be brought up again to the committee. This motion usually defeats the bill.
- *Postpone* or *Postpone to a Time Certain* Asks that a matter be brought before the body later or as a special order of business at a specific date and time.
- *Postpone Indefinitely* Asks to remove a bill from consideration, effectively defeating it. It is not subject to a motion to reconsider.
- *Privileged Motion* A motion that takes precedence for consideration.
- *Put Over* Put a measure aside until a future date without prejudice.
- *Recede* This motion asks the chamber of origin to adopt the

bill as amended by the other chamber. A refusal to recede, sometimes called to *insist,* results in defeating the bill or appointment of a conference committee.

- *Recess to a Time Certain* A motion to set the time and duration of recess and the time to reconvene.
- *Reconsider* A non-debatable motion that asks the body to reconsider its vote. It is often required immediately after a vote, or at least on the day the vote is challenged. Some states limit the maker of this motion to a legislator who voted on the prevailing side of the earlier vote.
- *Repass* Asks the chamber of origin to pass an engrossed bill as amended by the other chamber or conference committee.
- *Set Special Order* Asks to bring a matter promptly before the chamber as a special order of business.
- *Strike* or *Strike from the File or Folder* Asks to remove a bill from consideration, defeating it for the session.
- *Strike Out* or *Strike Out and Insert* Motions to remove a provision or remove a provision and add a new one. A motion to *strike the enacting* clause defeats a bill.
- *Strike Everything* or *Substitute* Requests the substitution of a new bill for the bill under consideration. The struck bill is defeated.
- *Substitution of Bill for Report* or *Substitution for an Adverse Report* This motion asks the chamber to reject a committee's recommendation to amend a bill and pass the original bill.
- *Suspend the Rules* A motion to set aside the rules that govern the chamber's action to allow what would otherwise be considered out of order. A super majority vote is usually required for adoption.
- *Take from the Table* A non-debatable motion to recall a bill that the committee had voted to no longer consider. It must be approved by a super majority vote and is not allowed in some states.

Officers Persons elected by the chamber or appointed by those elected by the chamber to perform the functions necessary to operate the chamber. The Senate President, Senate Secretary, House Speaker, and House Clerk are officers in all states. Other legislative officers may include the President pro tem, Speaker pro tem, and Parliamentarian. Other non-legislative officers may include the Sergeant-at-Arms, Legislative Counsel, Revisor of Statutes, Reading Clerk, and other support positions. Party positions such as floor leaders, whips, and caucus positions are officers in some states while in others are referred to as *unofficial officers* or *leaders.*

Order of Business The sequence of business according to the daily agenda for a chamber. The established order is found in the chamber's rules. The first order of business may be bill introduction and the sixteenth order of business may be other business. The order of business can be changed by super majority vote.

Orders Listings of bills to be acted upon and non-legal legislative works, such as memorials, resolves, and resolutions.

- *Consent Orders* After one reading, these are bills expected to pass on unanimous consent.
- *General Orders* or *Orders of the Day* Bills awaiting action by the Committee of the Whole or chamber and may be considered in any order that members desire. See *Calendar.*
- *Special Orders* Bills selected for consideration by unanimous consent; bills to be considered as special business on a specific date and time; bills scheduled for second reading.

Order, In and Out of An action is *in order,* and therefore valid, when it meets the chamber's parliamentary requirements. An action is *out of order*, and therefore invalid, when it violates procedure.

Override or Veto Override By a super majority vote of members in each and both chambers the legislature nullifies the effect of the Governor's veto and the enactment becomes an act.

Page A person, usually a student, who runs errands and performs other minor tasks to assist the legislature.

Parliamentary Inquiry A question of procedure posed by a member to the presiding officer during a committee meeting or floor session.

Pass or Passage Favorable action on a bill by a chamber. It is also used loosely to describe a committee's favorable report of a bill. *Final passage* is an affirmative vote taken at the conclusion of third reading.

Pass, Floor A pass approved by the leader of the chamber that allows a person who is not part of the chamber or its staff to go onto the area where the legislature, as a body, conducts its business. Issuance of floor passes may be stringently limited. Lobbyists are denied access to the floor when a chamber is in daily session.

Petition A formal request submitted to the legislature by citizens. In a state with a *right of free petition,* this is a citizen's request that the legislature consider enacting his or her bill.

Political Capital or Capital The intangible resources that can be applied to reach a desired legislative end. Political capital includes constituency, relationships, affinity, debts, favors, hope for support, and other factors that would cause a lawmaker to give a person or matter additional attention.

Political Committee or Political Action Committee (PAC) A group formed to make contributions to support issues or candidates who advance the issues that the PAC promotes. PACs must register with the state and periodically report their expenditures to the state.

Preamble The recitation of facts and public policy supporting a bill that appears before the enacting clause. It is a non-binding expression of *legislative intent* and does not appear in the codified law.

Pre-session A period prior to the regular session during which committees meet and proposed bills are considered. The chamber itself will not meet nor will chamber activities such as bill introductions take place. Pre-sessions allow part-time or citizen legislatures to carry on the work of the legislature, short of processing legislation, while the legislature is not in session.

Pre-session Filing The filing of a bill with the bill clerk before the first day of the annual legislative session. Pre-filed bills will be numbered and are automatically introduced on the first day of the regular session.

President of the Senate The presiding officer and the majority leader in states where a Senator is the President of the Senate. When the Lieutenant Governor is presiding, he or she is the President.

President pro tem(pore) The Senator who serves temporarily as the presiding officer in the absence of the President of the Senate. He or she is the majority party leader in states where the Lieutenant Governor presides over the Senate.

Procedure The rules of the chamber that govern its conduct. Procedure is found in published adopted joint rules, rules of the chamber, tradition, and manuals of parliamentary procedure.

Quorum In accord with chamber rules, the smallest number of members needed to conduct official business. Normally, a quorum is a simple majority of the members serving on a committee or in the chamber.

Quorum Call A message from the presiding officer requesting members to immediately attend a committee meeting or meeting of the entire chamber in order to establish a quorum.

Reading Presentation of a bill before the chamber. Bills receive three readings on three different days before the legislature or before each chamber, unless the readings are waived by a super majority vote. The actions that take place at each reading vary among the states, but generally include:

- *First Reading* The bill is introduced and referred to committee.
- *Second Reading* After the committee(s) of referral issues its report, the chamber debates, amends, and votes upon the bill.
- *Third Reading* The bill may or may not be debated or amended. It is voted upon for the third time and, if approved, is engrossed and sent to the other chamber for action.

Recess A temporary delay or pause in conducting official business by a committee or chamber. Also, a longer break during the session normally scheduled around holidays or elections.

- *Caucus recess* Called by the presiding officer to allow party members to break to caucus on a topic before the chamber or for the caucus to discipline an errant member.
- *Recess at the call of the chair* A very brief suspension of floor activity.

Referendum A proposal sent by the legislature to the voters proposing a constitutional amendment or other measure.

Refer or Referral Sending a bill to one or more committees for consideration.

- *Joint, Double,* or *Multiple* More than one committee has jurisdiction over a bill.
- *Sequential* One committee completes its review of a bill, then sends it to the next committee(s) of referral.
- *Split* The subject matter of the bill belongs to two or more committees who must meet together to review it.

Repeal To eliminate a law by enactment of a new law.

Report The formal response of a committee to the chamber regarding a bill that it has evaluated. As a noun, it refers to the compilation of the original bill, individual proposed amendments, a marked-up amended copy of the bill as recommended by the committee, the record of the roll call vote, a fiscal statement and a memorandum that explains the committee's deliberations, conclusions, rationale and recommendations. The majority and the minority on a committee may issue separate reports. At their simplest, the recommendations on a measure are *do pass* or *ought to pass* or a similar favorable recommendation, called a *favorable report; do pass as amended* or *ought to pass as amended* or a similar favorable recommendation that the bill should pass with proposed committee changes, also called a *favorable report; do not pass* or *ought not to pass* or a similar unfavorable recommendation, called an *unfavorable* or *adverse report.* As a verb, it means to send the report from a committee to the full chamber.

Requester A person other than a member of the legislature who requests a bill or other measure be taken up by the legislature.

Rescind Revocation of a previous action.

Resolution or Memorial A measure passed by one chamber (simple) or both chambers (joint or concurrent) adopting joint rules, expressing legislative opinion, congratulations, commendation, or sympathy, proposing a constitutional amendment, creating an interim committee, making requests to state agencies, urging that another governmental body do or not do something or a similar activity. Because it is not a law, it does not need the approval of the Governor.

Revise To insert new enactments into existing statutes.

Reviser or Revisor of Statutes The legislative services agency charged with, among other things, incorporating into statutes the acts of the legislature.

Rules The procedures followed by a committee or chamber. Most rules are adopted at the start of a legislative session.

- *Interim Rules* Govern a committee or chamber between the sessions.
- *Joint Rules* Are enacted by both chambers to govern their shared activities.
- *Senate Rules* or *House Rules* Govern the conduct of a chamber.
- *Special Rules* Rules temporarily adopted by the chamber to govern its consideration of a particular measure.
- *Uniform Joint Rules* Govern both chambers by the same rules.

Ruling of the Chair The decision of the presiding officer or committee chair on a matter of parliamentary practice.

Seating Chart The graphical depiction of the location of each member's seat or desk on the chamber floor.

Section A portion of the state codified law or a portion of a proposed measure.

Senate In a bicameral legislature, the smaller chamber. Members normally are elected by larger districts often for a longer term, usually four years. Nebraska has only a Senate.

Session The gathering of a chamber for official business.

- *Confirmation Session* Called to consider the Governor's proposed appointments over which the Senate has advice and consent authority.
- *Joint Session* Both chambers meet together in a non-legislating mode, e.g. to receive an address from the Governor or a dignitary.
- *Organizational Session* Held shortly after a general election to organize the chambers to do business.
- *Regular Session* The period during which the legislature meets, either the daily meeting or regularly scheduled or an extended annual term. The regular session occurs as mandated by the state constitution. Sessions can be *formal,* in which votes may be taken, or *informal,* in which discussion occurs but no votes are taken. The *session schedule* sets dates for floor periods, committee meetings, and deadlines for action by the body.
- *Special Session* or *Extraordinary Session* A convening of the legislature at a time other than during the regular session. A special session may be called by the Governor or by the legislature to consider the topics in the call for a session or as otherwise approved by a super majority of the legislature.
- *Veto Session* A special session called to review the Governor's vetoes.

Sine Die Adjournment Final adjournment. In some states sine die is a ceremonial rather than a substantive date. Sine die may occur at a convenient date well after the legislature has for all practical purposes ended its work for the year.

Single Subject The requirement that a proposed measure be limited to one subject. While determining whether a bill covers more than one subject may be difficult, the intent of the single subject requirement is to permit a legislator to vote for a bill without having to accept or reject an unrelated subject in the same bill.

Speaker The presiding officer of the House of Representatives or Delegates, Assembly, or Lower House.

Speaker pro tem(pore) The member who presides over the House in the absence of the Speaker.

Special Interest Non-legislators concerned with a matter before the legislature who as individuals or groups present their views and supporting information to lawmakers. Pejoratively, a description of those lobbying government for special benefits.

Sponsor See *Author.*

Staff Employees who assist the legislature in carrying out its duties. Full-time staff, sometimes called consultants or attaches, are supplemented by temporary staff such as pages during the legislative session. Partisan staff work for individual members and the party caucus. The legislative services agencies, and sometimes committee staff, are expected to be non-partisan. Staff include committee and personal staff, the Clerk or Secretary, Sergeant-at-Arms, and Chaplain, who in turn, supervise employees who report to them.

Stakeholders Those persons, companies, or groups who are not part of the legislature but who have a recognized interest in the outcome of legislation. Inclusion of stakeholders with substantial interests gives a sense of fairness to a bill, lessens political opposition, and increases political acceptability.

Statutes The compilation of laws maintained by the Secretary of State.

Subcommittee A subordinate, usually smaller subgroup of a full committee, composed of a few members of the full committee and given a specific charge or jurisdiction. A committee may have more than one subcommittee.

Sunset The predetermined time provided by a law at which a statute or one or more of its provisions ceases to be law. A self-repealing provision in a law.

Suspend or Suspension of the Rules Parliamentary procedure whereby the chamber can authorize itself to take actions that would otherwise be out of order. A super majority vote, normally two-thirds of those present, is required to adopt a motion to suspend the rules.

Suspense File A file into which is placed any bill costing the state more than a specified sum of money. After adoption of the state budget, suspense file bills are enacted as state resources permit.

Sustain The legislature's upholding of a Governor's veto by failing to gain enough votes to override the veto.

Testimony, Formal The taking of invited formal spoken comments by a committee, often accompanied by written submittals, from advocates, opponents, and executive agencies during a committee hearing. The information presented assists committee members in their deliberations on a bill before them. See *Comment, Public* or *Citizen*

Unanimous Consent A chamber may do anything procedural not denied to it by the constitution, its own rules notwithstanding, under unanimous consent. *Unanimous consent,* or the consent of all members, allows actions that would otherwise be out of order. A request for unanimous consent is defeated by a single member's objection.

Veto The limited constitutional power of a Governor to prevent a bill or part of a bill from becoming law. The veto can be nullified by a super majority vote of both chambers or a court of law.

- *Conditional Veto* The Governor sends the enactment back to the legislature with a list of amendments that must be made to avoid a veto.
- *Line Item Veto, Item Veto, Partial Veto,* or *Blue Pencil Veto* The Governor's rejection of a portion or portions of an appropriations bill.
- *People's Veto* The people repeal a law by referendum or initiative.
- *Pocket Veto* Occurs when a legislature has adjourned *sine die,* thus preventing reconsideration by the legislature.

Vote Formal statement of the will or decision of a legislator or a legislative body.

- *Division Vote* Counts each individual member through the raising of hands, standing in a line or otherwise being viewed and counted by the presiding officer. The total number of votes is reported, not the votes of each member.
- *En Bloc Vote* The disposition of several items, such as a series of bills or amendments, by taking one vote.
- *Free Vote* Floor leaders do not attempt to influence the direction of party members' votes.
- *Majority Vote* Sometimes called a *simple* or a *constitutional majority,* is half plus one of those voting in a quorum and is sufficient to conduct most business.

- *Roll Call Vote, Recorded Vote,* or *Yeas and Nays Vote* Each member is called by name and asked for a "yes" or "no" on the question. Electronic voting has greatly facilitated recorded votes of thc chamber.
- *Super Majority Vote* or *Extraordinary Vote* Three-fifths, two-thirds, three-fourths, four-fifths or unanimous, depending on the matter and rules of the chamber.
- *Voice Vote* or *Viva Voce* An oral "aye" or "no" vote with no official count taken. The presiding officer determines whether the "ayes" or "noes" carry by judging what he or she hears.
- *Vote Under the Gavel, Vote Without Objection,* or *Vote Under the Hammer* Approval is presumed unless objection is made prior to the presiding officer banging the gavel.

Vote Pairing, Pairs, or Pairings A procedure allowed in some chambers, whereby with permission of the chamber leader and before the vote is taken, a member announces that he or she has "paired" his or her vote with an opposing vote. One or both of the two members must be absent at the time of the vote. The two votes do not become part of the number of votes counted in enacting or defeating a measure.

Well In some bodies, the presiding officer's bench or the area directly in front of it or both.

Whip, Majority or Minority A party leader on the floor, one for the majority and one for the minority, responsible for assuring that their members vote according to direction by the party caucus or party leadership.

Withdraw To remove a bill, proposal, or question from consideration.

Work Session A committee meeting that works through a bill, measure, or resolve in order to issue a committee report.

Yield To surrender the floor temporarily to another member.

The following list gives the sources for most of the terms in the glossary:

Randall Gnant, *The Legislative Process in the Arizona Senate* (1996) http://www.azleg.state.az.us/bill3law.htm

California Legislature (1999)
http://www.leginfo.ca.gov/califleg.html

Colorado Capitol Connection, 1993 *Almanac Glossary* (1993)
http://www.capcon.com.html

Indiana House of Representatives, *Rules of the House of Representatives One Hundred Ninth General Assembly of Indiana* (1997)
http://www.state.in.us/legislative/rules.html

Iowa General Assembly, *A Glossary of Legislative and Budget Terms* (1994)
http://www.legis.state.ia.us/Central/LSB/Guides/gaguide.htm#pt8

Kentucky House of Representatives, *Glossary of Legislative Terms* (1997)
http://www.irc.state.ky.us/leg_proc/glossary.htm
Louisiana Legislature, *Legislative Terms* (1997)
http://www.legis.state.la.us/terms.htm

Lawmaking in Massachusetts (1997)
http://www.magnet.state.ma.us/legis/lawmkng.htm
Maine 118th Legislature, *Glossary* (1997)
http://www.state.me.us/legis/opla/glossary.htm

Michigan Legislature, *Glossary of Legislative Terms* (1997)
http://michiganlegislature.org/isapi/nls_ax.dll/glossary

Minnesota State Legislature, *Legislative Terms and Definitions* (1991)
http://www.revisor.leg.state.mn.us/stats/645/

Nevada House, *Common Terms of the Legislature* (1997)
http://www.leg.state.nv.us/general/terms.htm

Notes